What's the Least I Can Believe and Still Be a Christian?

New Edition with Study Guide

What's the Least I Can Believe and Still Be a Christian?

New Edition with Study Guide

A Guide to What Matters Most

MARTIN THIELEN

WESTMINSTER
JOHN KNOX PRESS
LOUISVILLE · KENTUCKY

© 2011, 2013 Martin Thielen

Second edition
Published by Westminster John Knox Press
Louisville, Kentucky

13 14 15 16 17 18 19 20 21 22 — 10 9 8 7 6 5 4 3 2 1

Book design by Drew Stevens
Cover design by designpointinc.com

Except where otherwise noted, Scripture quotations are from the New Revised Standard Version of the Bible, copyright © 1989 by the Division of Christian Education of the National Council of the Churches of Christ in the U.S.A., and are used by permission.

Scripture quotations marked NIV are from the Holy Bible, New International Version. Copyright © 1973, 1978, 1984 International Bible Society. Used by permission of Zondervan Bible Publishers.

Scripture quotations marked NKJV are from The New King James Version. Copyright © 1979, 1980, 1982, Thomas Nelson Inc., Publishers.

Library of Congress Cataloging-in-Publication Data
Thielen, Martin
  What's the least I can believe and still be a Christian? : a guide to what matters most : new edition with study guide / Martin Thielen. — Second edition.
    pages cm
  ISBN 978-0-664-23938-1 (alk. paper)
1. Jesus Christ — Person and offices. 2. Christianity — Essence, genius, nature. I. Title.
  BT103.T455 2013
  232'.8 — dc23

                                                                      2012039827

Most Westminster John Knox Press books are available at special quantity
discounts when purchased in bulk by corporations, organizations, and special-
interest groups. For more information, please e-mail SpecialSales@wjkbooks.com.

To the congregation and staff at First United Methodist Church,
Lebanon, Tennessee, who for a
decade joined me in proclaiming a vibrant
mainline faith of "Open Hearts, Open Minds,
and Open Doors" to our community.
As Paul said to the church at Philippi,
"I thank my God upon every remembrance of you."

CONTENTS

INTRODUCTION
TO THE NEW EDITION

∽∾

When I wrote *What's the Least I Can Believe and Still Be a Christian? A Guide to What Matters Most*, I expected to be criticized by religious-right fundamentalists. That expectation was met, including by people who accused me of promoting watered-down, minimalist Christianity. These folks obviously read the title but not the book. One infuriated reader wrote me a long e-mail, telling me that my book "would send large numbers of people to hell." I was taken to task by a Christian talk-radio host who blasted me for "not believing the Bible." I tried to nuance the difference between believing the Bible, which I do, and believing in strict biblical literalism, which I don't. But he was not interested in having that discussion. A fundamentalist pastor in my community preached an entire sermon series against my book for his congregation, which was not far from my church. Several religious-right believers posted negative reviews about the book on Amazon and various blogs. However, since I fully expected these kinds of responses, they did not particularly bother me or surprise me, although I was grateful that scathing negative responses were relatively few.

What did surprise me was the huge amount of overwhelmingly positive responses I received about the book.

Clearly, *What's the Least I Can Believe and Still Be a Christian?* struck a chord with large numbers of people. Here are a few examples:

- I received e-mails from college students who thanked me for the book, including one who said, "It helped me make sense of my faith."
- A young adult recently e-mailed me to say that the book "helped confirm my call into vocational ministry."
- I received numerous letters from people who said that they were agnostics or atheists but enjoyed the book anyway. One said, "If I were a Christian, I would feel at home in your church." Several told me that they were now rethinking their atheism.
- Dozens of people shared with me profoundly personal stories about their faith struggles and how the book helped them on their journey. One person said, "Your book helped me embrace the God I always wanted to believe in."
- I heard from many readers who thanked me for making the Christian faith accessible to laypeople. One person wrote, "Thank you for articulating theology in a way that doesn't require a theological degree to understand."
- Numerous people told me that the book helped them reclaim their faith. One person said, "This is the book I've been waiting to find for the last twenty years. It helped me realize that I'm not alone in questioning beliefs I have struggled with my entire life. Thank you for helping me find my way back to God."
- Dozens of pastors wrote, telling me that they used the book for small-group studies in their churches, or that they followed the seven-week, congregation-wide initiative based on the book, with positive results. One pastor said, "This is the best church study we've ever experienced, with large numbers of people participat-

ing. Thank you!" Another said, "Your book is a splendid description of a faith that is open-minded but not so open that one's brains fall out." One pastor e-mailed, "Your book is both accessible and yet profound. It served as a great tool for our congregation." A pastor at a large congregation told me that his church gave out copies of the book to guests at their Christmas Eve services.

- Many people wrote asking if I knew where they could find a church that affirmed the theology found in my book. One of them said, "If I could find a church that agrees with your book, I would attend every Sunday."
- My favorite response was, "Excellent theology, writing, and storytelling. I hope the book gets a huge following and is reprinted a jillion times."

The overwhelming positive response to *What's the Least I Can Believe and Still Be a Christian?* along with its strong sales record, tells me that there is a deep hunger in America for a viable alternative to closed-minded faith. Soon after writing the book, I watched an interesting episode of the popular television show *Glee*. In this episode several high school students explain why they are turned off by organized religion. From their perspective, the church is down on gays, women, and science. When you add to that the arrogant and judgmental attitudes found in many religious-right churches, it's easy to see why religion repels so many people. If the only faith options are fundamentalism or no religion, many people will opt for no religion.

Thankfully, a better alternative exists—vibrant, centrist, open-minded, grace-filled, gender-equal, life-giving, moderate/mainline faith. That's the message behind *What's the Least I Can Believe and Still Be a Christian? A Guide to What Matters Most.* Although the book was written for individual readers, for both seekers and believers, it was also written for moderate and mainline churches. Therefore, I am delighted that Westminster John Knox Press decided to publish this new edition of the book. This edition includes a comprehensive Study Guide for implementing a seven-week, worship and small-group based, congregation-wide initiative built on the book. This seven-week initiative can help moderate and mainline churches better tell their story to their own members, as well as to unchurched people in their communities. The Study Guide provides church leaders with everything they need to carry out the event, including promotional tools, guidelines for small-group leaders, and worship and sermon ideas.

We in the moderate/mainline tradition have a compelling faith story to tell. However, we need practical resources to better share that story. This new edition of *What's the Least I Can Believe and Still Be a Christian?* will help you do so boldly. May God's blessings be with you as you read and study and share this book with others. Before long, I plan to write a follow-up book called *The Answer to Bad Religion Is Not No Religion, but Good Religion.* I hope you will be on the lookout for it!

Martin Thielen

Brentwood, Tennessee
2013

PREFACE

When I first met Danny, he said, "Preacher, you need to know that I'm an atheist. I don't believe the Bible. I don't like organized religion. And I can't stand self-righteous, judgmental Christians."

In spite of Danny's avowed atheism and my devout Christian beliefs, we became close friends. Over the next year Danny and I engaged in numerous conversations about God, religion, and faith. During that time Danny softened his stance on atheism. One day, after a long conversation, he announced with a laugh, "I've decided to upgrade from an atheist to an agnostic." Several months later Danny said, "I've had an epiphany. I realize that I don't reject Christianity. Instead, I reject the way that intolerant Christians *package* Christianity." A few weeks after that conversation, Danny said, "Martin, you've just about convinced me on this religion stuff. So I want to know—what's the least I can believe and still be a Christian?"

"What's the least I can believe and still be a Christian?" What a great question! This little book represents my best effort to answer that question. Part 1 presents ten things Christians *don't* need to believe. In short, Christians don't need to believe in closed-minded faith. For example, Christians don't need to believe that Jews are going to hell or that it's heresy to believe in evolution. Part 2 presents ten things Christians *do* need to believe—what matters most, if you will. They need to believe in Jesus—his life, teachings, example, death, and resurrection. A great benefit of these beliefs is that they provide promising answers to life's most profound questions, including Where is God? What brings fulfillment? What about suffering? And is there hope? Like Danny, many people in the twenty-first century hunger for an alternative expression of Christian faith that's different from the judgmental and narrow-minded caricatures they see on religious television and in the news. This book offers such an alternative. It articulates centrist, mainline, and moderate Christianity in a way that's fresh and easy to understand. It also offers authentic Christian insights that speak to our deepest human needs. So turn the page, and let's begin exploring Danny's interesting question: "What's the least I can believe and still be a Christian?"

PART 1

∽◦◦∽

TEN THINGS CHRISTIANS
DON'T NEED TO BELIEVE

You've probably heard the old gospel song called "Gimme That Old-Time Religion." The chorus says, "Gimme that old-time religion, gimme that old-time religion, gimme that old-time religion, it's good enough for me." Well, a lot of old-time religion is good and noble, and we'll explore much of it in part 2 of this book. But some old-time religion is neither good nor noble. Old-time religion gave us the Crusades, the Inquisition, and religious wars. Old-time religion oppressed women, defended slavery, and stifled scientific inquiry. The fact is, some of that old-time religion is unhealthy and needs to be discarded. In the chapters that follow, we will review ten tenets of old-time religion that Christians can and should discard.

CHAPTER 1

⟡

GOD CAUSES CANCER, CAR WRECKS, AND OTHER CATASTROPHES

Those eighteen who were killed when the tower of Siloam fell on them—do you think that they were worse offenders than all the others living in Jerusalem? No, I tell you.

—Jesus, in Luke 13:2, 3–5

One summer afternoon a country preacher went to visit a farmer in his congregation. As the preacher and farmer sipped iced tea and talked, the farmer's son bolted into the house, carrying a dead cat by the tail. In his excitement the boy did not notice the preacher sitting on the other side of the room. He rushed up to his father, held up the dead cat, and said, "Dad! I found this stray cat in the barn. I hit him with a board, then I threw him against the barn, then I kicked him, and then I stomped him." At that moment the boy saw the preacher. Without missing a beat, he said, "And then, Pastor, the Lord called him home."

God often gets blamed for things God does not do. When I was a teenager, a friend of mine named Rick died

3

in a car wreck. Rick, a delightful young man and deeply committed Christian, had planned to become a minister. At his funeral the pastor said, "Although we cannot understand it, God's will has been done." Even though I was only sixteen years old and a new Christian, I knew better. God didn't kill my friend Rick: a drunk driver did.

Just last week a young police officer from middle Tennessee lost his life in a traffic accident. His police chief said, "Not knowing how the good Lord makes his decisions sometimes, we were all caught off guard by Jeremy's sudden demise." But it wasn't the good Lord's decision that killed this young man. It was the driver of a pickup truck who ran a red light. If God had actually been the one who killed this fine young policeman, God would not be a "good Lord" at all.

Unfortunately, people attribute awful events to God all the time. A child dies of leukemia, and people say, "God wanted another angel in heaven." A young woman dies of breast cancer, leaving behind a husband and young children, and people say, "God works in mysterious ways." A fifty-year-old man works twelve hours a day, seven days a week, chain smokes, eats unhealthy food, and never exercises. He then suffers a deadly heart attack, and people say, "The Lord knows best." On their prom night two teenagers die in a car wreck, and people say, "God must have had a purpose."

An extreme example of blaming tragedy on God happened after September 11, 2001. Several days after the terrorist attack on New York City, a well-known television preacher claimed that 9/11 was God's retribution for America's sins. He said that abortionists, feminists, gays, lesbians, and the ACLU had angered God so much that God used the terrorists to punish America. I doubt that theory would go over very well with the families of the victims. Years earlier the same preacher claimed that God created AIDS to punish homosexuals. Try telling that to the young hemophiliac in my congregation who suffered and then died from AIDS after receiving a contaminated blood transfusion. Or try telling that to children born with AIDS or spouses who get AIDS because their husband or wife was unfaithful. Or for that matter, try telling homosexual men or women, created in the image of God and loved by Jesus, that God gave them AIDS to punish them for their sexual orientation.

A more-recent example of blaming God for tragedy came after the devastating 2010 earthquake in Haiti. One well-known religious leader suggested that Haiti's suffering was the result of a voodoo "pact with the devil" that Haitian slaves had made two hundred years earlier, during their rebellion against French colonization. That bizarre theory strongly implies that God sent the devastating earthquake to Haiti as a punishment for their past sins. It's beyond my comprehension how Christians can believe that God would purposely annihilate over two hundred thousand people for any reason, much less to punish a poverty-stricken nation for a two-hundred-year-old sin. We need to be careful about attributing terrorist attacks, disease, earthquakes, or other catastrophes to God.

Acts of God?

Last year tornadoes ravaged several communities in my home state of Tennessee. The next night on the evening news, a local official from one of the hardest-hit communities called the tornado "an act of God." When people and property are destroyed in tornadoes, earthquakes, tsunamis, and cyclones, we often refer to it as "an act of God." But do we really want to believe that? When a tornado rips through a trailer park and kills little children, or a devastating earthquake kills massive numbers of people, do we really believe that is an act of God? An act of nature, yes. But an act of God? How can we worship a God like that? How can we love and serve a God who inflicts cancer on children, wipes out teenagers in car wrecks, destroys families in tornadoes, or kills hundreds of thousands of people in a tsunami or earthquake?

Christians don't have to believe that. Christians should *not* believe that! The God of Jesus Christ, who placed children on his lap and blessed them, does not go around killing people with tornadoes, earthquakes, cancer, and automobile accidents. God does not have a weekly quota of malignant tumors to distribute, heart attacks to pass out, or battlefield wounds to inflict.

Just because something bad happens does not mean God causes it to happen. Jesus understood that. We see an example in Luke 13:4–5. Although we don't know the details, eighteen laborers were killed in Jerusalem in an apparent construction accident. People in Jesus' day assumed that God caused the accident, presumably to punish the workers for their sin. Jesus rejected that idea and so must we. In response to this tragedy, Jesus says, "Those eighteen who were killed when the tower of Siloam fell on them—do you think that they were worse offenders than all the others living in Jerusalem? No, I tell you." God didn't cause that tragedy back then, and God doesn't cause tragedies today.

Years ago a woman in my congregation lost her teenage son, Daniel, in a tragic car wreck. At first she felt bitter toward God. Overwhelmed by grief, she said, "I hate God for taking Daniel away from me." Several months later this woman came to realize that God did not "take" her son. With keen theological insight she told me, "It's not God's fault that Daniel is dead. God did not create cars and highways. Daniel's death was just a terrible accident. God did not *take* Daniel. Instead, God *received* him when he came."

Bringing Good Out of Bad

God does not cause cancer, car wrecks, or other catastrophes. God is not the author of suffering. However, that does not mean that God cannot redeem suffering; God can and God does. In fact, God brings good things out of tragedy all the time. For example, take Daniel's mother mentioned above. Whenever anyone in her community loses a child, she's always there. She empathizes with their pain, grieves with them, and helps them walk through their nightmare. In mercy God brought something good out of that sad story. But that does *not* mean God caused the tragedy. As God tells a grieving father in the bestselling novel *The Shack,* "Just because I work incredible good out of unspeakable tragedies doesn't mean I orchestrate the tragedies."[1]

Suffering is a complex issue for Christian believers and has no simple solutions. We will deal with the problem of suffering in more depth in part 2 of this book. But for now it's enough to affirm that God does not cause pain and suffering. The idea that God does cause pain and suffering is "old-time religion" that Christians can and should abandon.

Many years ago, a few months after I arrived at a new church, I went to visit an inactive member of my congregation. Although he used to attend church regularly, after his wife died, he quit coming. By the time I arrived at the church, he had not attended worship for several years. During our visit I said, "The congregation and I would love for you and your children to return to church."

"Thanks for the invitation," he replied, "but I don't believe in God anymore."

"Tell me about the God you don't believe in," I said.

So he told me his story. Years earlier, he, his wife, and their two young children came to church every Sunday. But then his wife developed breast cancer. In spite of all their prayers and the best medical treatment available, she only got worse. He begged God to save her, but she died anyway. He told me, "When I buried my wife, I also buried my faith. I don't believe in a God who kills twenty-eight-year-old mothers with cancer."

I replied, "I don't believe in that kind of God either."

❊ ❊ ❊

Bottom line: *Although God can and does bring good results out of tragedy, God does not cause tragic events to occur.*

Note for Chapter 1

1. William P. Young, *The Shack: A Novel* (Newbury Park, CA: Windblown Media, 2007), 185.

CHAPTER 2

⬠⬠

GOOD CHRISTIANS
DON'T DOUBT

I believe; help my unbelief!
—the father of the convulsing boy, in Mark 9:24

Several years ago Hollywood produced a powerful film called *Cinderella Man*, starring Russell Crowe and Renée Zellweger. If you're not familiar with the movie, *Cinderella Man* tells the true story of Jim Braddock, a boxer during the Depression years. After injuring his hand, Jim's boxing career came to an end. Unable to find regular work, Jim and his family struggled greatly during the Depression years. Although a devout Roman Catholic, those bleak years strained Jim's faith in God. In one poignant scene of the movie, the Braddock family had no money, the kids were sick, the electricity had been cut off in their apartment, and they had little food.

Late that evening, Jim came home after another unsuccessful day of seeking work. The kids were in bed, coughing with a bad cold; the apartment was freezing; and the only light in the apartment came from a candle. Jim sat down at the table with his wife to eat a meager bite of dinner. He and his wife joined hands and bowed their heads to say a blessing over the tiny meal. She began the prayer, "Lord, we are grateful . . . ," but Jim did not join her. She looked up at him, and with her eyes asked, "What's the matter? Why are you not praying with me?" For a moment Jim looked at her in silence. Then he said, "I'm all prayed out."

All Prayed Out

Have you ever felt all prayed out? Do you ever have doubts about God? Do you ever wonder if God really exists? Or, if God does exist, do you ever wonder if God is as good, loving, and just as you have been taught? If so, you are in good company. People have felt all prayed out for centuries, including many biblical heroes.

After years of praying for a child with no results, Abraham and Sarah felt all prayed out. Frustrated with leading the people of Israel through the wilderness, Moses felt all prayed out. Sick in mind, body, and spirit, Job felt all prayed out. Hiding for his life in a desert cave, his enemies in hot pursuit, David felt all prayed out. Crying out to God in anger and anguish, the prophet Jeremiah felt all prayed out. Believing that God had abandoned him, the psalmist felt all prayed out. After denying Jesus three times, Peter felt all prayed out. After repeatedly praying for healing but not receiving it, the apostle Paul felt all prayed out. In anguish over his inability to believe that Jesus was alive, Thomas felt all prayed out.

At one point in his life, even Jesus felt all prayed out. The authorities were breathing down his neck. Powerful people wanted him dead. He had less than a day to live. So he went to the Garden of Gethsemane to pray. Three times Jesus poured out his soul to God to spare his life. "Father," he pleaded, "Don't let me die; let me live!" But the heavens were silent. Instead of being rescued by God, Jesus was arrested, abandoned by his disciples, denied by his best friend, put on trial, condemned, beaten, mocked, and cruelly executed. Hanging on the cross, Jesus cried out, "My God, my God, why have you forsaken me?" Like so many others through the years, Jesus felt all prayed out.

Some people believe that religious questions, struggles, and doubts are a sin—but they are wrong. Doubt is not the enemy of faith but part of faith. Tennyson was right when he said, "There lives more faith in honest doubt, believe me, than in half the creeds." When author Madeleine L'Engle was asked, "Do you believe in God without any doubts?" she replied, "I believe in God with all my doubts." Her response reminds me of a profound passage in the Bible that says, "Lord, I believe; help my unbelief!" (Mark 9:24 NKJV). Most of us can relate to that. We do believe, but we also have times of unbelief. That's always been true for people of faith, and it always will be.

But Some Doubted

Take, for example, the resurrection of Christ. Most people would agree that belief in the resurrection is the heartbeat of Christian faith. But when God raised Jesus from the dead, skepticism about his resurrection abounded. In fact, doubts about the resurrection are recorded in all four Gospels. When the early followers of Christ heard the glorious news of the resurrection, they struggled to believe it. Matthew 28 says, "When they saw him [after the resurrection], they worshiped him; *but some doubted*" (v. 17, with added emphasis). Mark 16 says, "When they heard that he [Jesus] was alive and had been seen by her [Mary

Magdalene] *they would not believe it*" (v. 11, with added emphasis). Luke 24 says, "Returning from the tomb, they told all this [about the resurrection] to the eleven and to all the rest. . . . *But these words seemed to them an idle tale, and they did not believe them*" (v. 9, 11, with added emphasis). John 20 says, "The other disciples told him [Thomas], 'We have seen the Lord.' But he said to them, '*Unless I see the mark of the nails in his hands, and put my finger in the mark of the nails and my hand in his side, I will not believe*'" (v. 25, with added emphasis). Skepticism, doubt, and uncertainty exist in all four Gospel accounts of the resurrection. Eventually Christ's followers affirmed faith in his resurrection, but they had to work through their doubts, questions, and struggles to get there.

I had my first serious struggle with religious doubt during college. I did not grow up in church but became a Christian believer during my sophomore year in high school. For three years my church nurtured me in an ultra-conservative, intensely emotional version of Christianity. My church was heavy on heart religion but light on head religion. Then I went off to college. For the first time in my life, I had serious discussions with agnostics and even atheists. I studied philosophy, world religions, and evolutionary biology. I was also introduced to critical academic study of the Bible and advanced theology. My professors taught me things I never heard in Sunday school.

My simple, conservative, emotion-based Christian faith was seriously challenged. In that setting I struggled deeply with my faith. I grappled with hard questions like, If God is all-loving and all-powerful, why is there so much suffering and evil in the world? I wondered, How can I reconcile my belief in science with my belief in the Bible? My simplistic "Love Jesus with all your heart" religion was not adequate anymore. For a while I thought I was losing my faith. I shared my struggles with my college advisor and mentor. At the conclusion of our visit, he handed me a book written by an Episcopal priest called *Honest to God*. There's little in that book I would agree with today, but at the time it served as bread for a hungry beggar. In many ways that book saved my faith and my vocation as a minister. It taught me that doubt is not the enemy of faith but part of faith. It taught me that it is OK to ask hard questions about God, that you can be a thinking person and still be a Christian, and that science and religion are compatible with each other. Since that difficult faith struggle during college, I've learned that it's OK to say, along with the great heroes of the Bible, "Lord, I believe; help my unbelief!"

❀   ❀   ❀

Bottom line: *Doubt is not the enemy of faith but part of authentic Christianity.*

CHAPTER 3

⌒⌒⌒

TRUE CHRISTIANS CAN'T
BELIEVE IN EVOLUTION

In the beginning God created the heavens and the earth.

—Genesis 1:1 NIV

Back in the 1990s I pastored a church in Honolulu. The church was located near Waikiki beach, so I kept a surfboard in my office and another at my house. As the old saying goes, "It's a tough job, but someone has to do it!"

My congregation included a large number of seekers, people who had not yet become Christians but who were exploring the Christian faith. Most had Buddhist backgrounds. Many of those seekers were students at the University of Hawaii. One of them, a young woman named Mary, was working on her PhD in biology. After attending our church for over a year, Mary asked for an appointment with me. On the one hand Mary felt drawn to Christianity. But on the other hand she struggled with the issue of science and faith, especially evolution. She told me, "I want to believe in God, but a literal reading of Genesis is impossible for me. As badly as I want to be a Christian, I cannot forfeit my mind in the process." Mary wanted to know if she could reconcile her belief in evolution with her belief in the Bible, especially the book of Genesis. I will never forget her question: "Dr. Thielen, can I be a scientist *and* a Christian?"

Scientific Creationism

Although an oversimplification, two major options exist for Christian believers concerning God's creation of the universe. The first position is called "scientific creationism." This view, held by many conservative Christians, insists on an extremely literal reading of Genesis 1–2 to explain the details of creation. Although several versions of scientific creationism exist, the most popular (young-earth creationism) says the world was created in six literal twenty-four-hour days. Based on biblical genealogies, it argues that the world is less than ten thousand years old. It claims that Adam and Eve were actual historical figures, not descendants of other creatures.

This theory rejects the scientific view that fossils were formed over millions of years. Instead, it claims that fossils were created in just a few weeks by the worldwide flood described in Genesis 6–9. Although this view allows for minor changes in species over the years, it completely rejects the possibility that one species evolved into another. In a nutshell, scientific creationism argues that evolution is a myth, a lie, and an enemy of faith.

Many sincere, well-meaning, God-fearing people affirm scientific creationism, and I respect these people. However, this position has major problems. First, it has *scientific* problems. It denies virtually every branch of modern science, including physics, chemistry, cosmology, geology, anthropology, genetics, and biology. From a scientific perspective, creation science is seriously flawed.

Not only does this literalist approach have scientific problems; it also has *biblical* problems. Contrary to what this view teaches, the Bible is not a science book. Scripture was written in a prescientific age. The book of Genesis was never written to give us a scientific explanation of creation. It is not a book of astronomy, geology, and biology. Genesis is not interested in protons, DNA structure, radioactive decay, and geological strata.

Genesis doesn't try to teach us *how* God created but *that* God created. In fact, Genesis has two completely different creation stories, one in Genesis 1:1–2:3 and another in Genesis 2:4–25. The two accounts don't agree with each other and cannot be reconciled. For example, in the first account man and woman are created last, but in the second account the man is created first. So what's the deal? The deal is that the Bible cares little about science and very much about theology. Scripture doesn't address or care about scientific details of creation. Instead, the Bible is concerned with more-important subjects like God, faith, meaning, love, justice, ethics, and hope.

Beyond the obvious scientific and biblical problems with scientific creationism, its biggest flaw is that it forces people to make an either/or choice between science and faith, a totally unnecessary choice. Of course you may believe scientific creationism; many good Christian people do. But if so, you need to be honest about the serious scientific and biblical challenges that come with this view, grapple with them, and come to an acceptable resolution in your mind.

Theistic Evolution

A second, more-promising Christian position concerning creation is called "theistic evolution." Theistic evolution affirms, along with science, that the universe was created through some kind of evolutionary process. However, unlike atheism, this view believes that God directed that process. This position claims that God created the universe but did so through the process of evolution. Theistic evolution is the overwhelming position of scientists who are also believers. A good example of this view can be found in an excellent book by Dr. Francis Collins: *The Language of God: A Scientist Presents Evidence for Belief.*[1] Theistic evolution was the position of the late Pope John Paul II and is taught by the Roman Catholic Church. It's also the position of most mainline Christians. Theistic evolution provides a satisfying synthesis of science and faith that makes sense for millions of Christian believers.

Years ago a conservative pastor asked me, "Do you believe in creationism, or do you believe in evolution?"

"Yes," I said.

He gave me a strange look and said, "What do you mean, 'Yes'?"

I said, "Yes, I believe in creationism. And yes, I believe in evolution. I believe God created the world, but I believe God created through evolution."

He was not happy with that answer, and you may not be happy with that answer either. That's OK. Good Christians disagree on this issue. But for millions of Christians, theistic evolution is the only option that makes both spiritual and scientific sense.

Several years ago, the state of Kansas fought a major battle over the teaching of evolution in the public school system. Of course, that battle is not new. Way back in 1925, evolution was hotly debated in a Tennessee courtroom. A public school teacher named John Scopes was put on trial for violating a state law against teaching evolution in public schools. They called it the "Scopes Monkey Trial." During the proceedings battle lines were drawn; no middle ground existed. You either believed in godless, atheistic evolution — or else you believed in God, Christianity, and the Bible.

Hollywood made a movie about that trial, which became a classic, called *Inherit the Wind*, starring Spencer Tracy and Gene Kelly. In the closing scene of the movie, the attorney who defended John Scopes for teaching evolution was picking up his things from a table, including two books. The first book was *The Origin of Species* by Charles Darwin, which first laid out the theory of evolution. The second book was the Bible. The attorney picked up Darwin's *Origin of Species* and then set it down. Then he picked up the Bible and set it down. Back and forth he went, holding one book, then the other. Which to choose? Biology or Genesis? Reason or faith? Science or Spirit? Finally the attorney picked up *both* books, Darwin's *Origin of Species* and the Bible, tucked them under his arm, and walked out of the courtroom.

And so Mary, the young biology PhD student, asked me, "Can I be a scientist *and* a Christian?" The answer is yes—a thousand times yes!

❊ ❊ ❊

Bottom line: *Science and faith are fully compatible, and theistic evolution is a perfectly acceptable Christian belief.*

Note for Chapter 3

1. Francis Collins, *The Language of God: A Scientist Presents Evidence for Belief* (New York: Free Press, 2006).

CHAPTER 4

⸺ ◌◌◌ ⸺

WOMEN CAN'T BE PREACHERS AND MUST SUBMIT TO MEN

There is neither Jew nor Greek, slave nor free, male nor female, for you are all one in Christ Jesus.

                         —Paul, in Galatians 3:28 NIV

One of the saddest realities of religious fundamentalism is how it treats women. We are all familiar with the oppression of women in certain Middle Eastern countries. In many places in the world, woman can't drive, vote, or leave home without a male escort. And when they do venture out, they must cover their entire bodies with a burka. Women who disobey these rigid gender laws risk beatings and even death at the hands of vicious religious fundamentalists. And it's all done in the name of God.

Obviously things are different in America. Yet even here religion sometimes oppresses women. For example, many Christian churches tell women that God requires them to submit to their husbands. Several years ago a large Protestant denomination in America passed church legislation requiring women to "graciously submit" to their husbands. Where does this backward idea come from?

A Return to Slavery?

Proponents of this view claim that it comes from the Bible. For example, in Ephesians 5, Paul writes, "Wives, submit to your husbands" (v. 22 NIV). Some conservative Christians look at that verse and say, "Case closed: women must submit to men." But in the very next chapter of Ephesians, Paul also writes, "Slaves, obey your earthly masters" (6:5 NIV). We obviously don't promote slavery anymore, so why would anyone in the twenty-first century promote the submission of women?

When Paul wrote these words about marriage, the world was totally dominated by men. In Paul's day women were considered property of their fathers or husbands. And when Paul wrote these words about slavery, slave ownership was totally accepted as a way of life. People were not yet questioning the ethics of slavery. Paul was a part of that culture, and that worldview is reflected in his writings. But even in that ancient culture, Paul knew that God's great dream for humanity is equality. Paul wrote that vision down in one of his letters. In Galatians 3, Paul says, "There is neither Jew nor Greek, slave nor free, male nor female, for you are all one in Christ Jesus" (v. 28 NIV). This passage pulsates with God's desire to see all people free and equal. God doesn't want people to be in the bondage of slavery. Nor does God want women to be submissive, second-class citizens. God intends for marriage to be a partnership, not a hierarchy.

What's true in the home is also true in the church. Women are perfectly capable of holding leadership positions in church, including pastoral positions, and should be allowed to exercise that authority. Unfortunately, that's not always the case. In fact, most churches in America do not allow women to serve as clergy. That's obviously the case in the Roman Catholic Church, but it's also true in most Protestant churches. For example, the Southern Baptist Convention absolutely forbids women to serve as clergy. If a Southern Baptist church hires a woman as pastor, that church is promptly kicked out of the local denominational association. However, this "no women allowed" policy is not limited to Catholics and Southern Baptists. Most churches in America do not allow women to serve as pastors.

Stopping at Half-Court

This negative attitude toward women in ministry reminds me of girls' basketball back in my high school days. Young readers might not believe me, but back in the 1970s, girls were not allowed to play full-court basketball; they could only play half-court. Back then people actually believed that women were too delicate to play full-court basketball. They thought that women did not have the stamina and endurance to play a full-court game. Although that seems absurd to us today, that's how it used to be. Sadly a lot of churches still follow that half-court rule. They allow women to play but only half-court. They allow women to teach children's Sunday school. They let them sing in the choir. They might even let them serve as children's direc- tor. And they are more than happy to take women's money. But once women get to half-court, they have to stop. They can't chair the finance committee, the building and grounds committee, or the personnel committee. Neither can they serve as deacons. And they surely can't be preachers.

Thankfully, that's not the case in most mainline tradi- tions, including United Methodist, Lutheran, Episcopal,

Presbyterian, Disciples of Christ, United Church of Christ, and American Baptist denominations. In mainline churches, women don't have to stop at half-court. Instead, they play significant leadership roles. That's certainly true in my congregation. Our lay leader is a woman. The chair of our staff parish relations committee is a woman. Women serve on all our committees and chair many of them. Our business administrator is a woman. Our minister of education is a woman. Our previous music minister was a woman. It's just a matter of time before the senior pastor will be a woman. However, they will have to get rid of me first! The United Methodist Church has a large and rapidly growing number of female clergy. We also have a growing number of female district superintendents and bishops. The same dynamics are true in many other mainline and moderate denominations.

Years ago, when I was still in the Southern Baptist church, I was a strong advocate for women clergy, and I have the battle scars to prove it. In fact, my church ordained women to the gospel ministry, which deeply upset some of my conservative colleagues. Although I greatly appreciate the many wonderful gifts my old denomination gave me, I finally left the Southern Baptist Convention in 1994. One of the primary reasons I left was their total rejection of women in pastoral leadership. The following year, as I was making a final decision about which denomination to join, I received a brochure in the mail from the United Methodist Church. A routine recruiting brochure tried to attract young people to a career in ministry. The brochure was full of pictures of United Methodist clergy and young people. At least half of the pictures were of women. I could hardly believe my eyes! Women were being invited, even recruited, to become United Methodist clergypersons.

I wept when I saw that brochure. I thought about all the women I knew in my old denomination who were called by God to be ministers, who were gifted for ministry, and who were educated for ministry but were rejected solely because of their gender. A few months after receiving that brochure, I had a meeting with the cabinet (the bishop and the district superintendents) to discuss my transfer to the United Methodist Church.

"Martin," they asked me, "why do you want to become a United Methodist?"

I replied, "There are many reasons why I want to join this denomination." Then I held up that brochure and said, "Here is one of the most important."

Of course, United Methodists, along with other mainline denominations, still need to make progress concerning women in ministry. For example, more women need to become senior pastors of larger congregations. But we've come a long way in this area, and we continue to make progress. I believe this pleases God greatly.

When I think about women in the life of the church, I'm reminded of an old classic Peanuts cartoon. Charlie Brown has just been beaten in a game of baseball by Lucy. One of Charlie's friends chides him for losing to "a mere girl." Charlie Brown responds, "Girls aren't as mere as they used to be."

✿　✿　✿

Bottom line: *Women are fully equal with men in marriage, in church, and in society.*

CHAPTER 5

⊂⊙⊃

GOD CARES ABOUT SAVING SOULS BUT NOT ABOUT SAVING TREES

Let justice roll down like waters,
and righteousness like an everflowing stream.

—Amos 5:24

In the fall of 1982, five months after graduating from seminary, I was invited to speak at a gathering of conservative evangelical pastors. After careful deliberation I chose to speak on the subject of environmental stewardship. Standing before one hundred preachers, Bible in hand, I passionately shared my conviction that God profoundly cares about the environment and expects the church to engage actively in responsible stewardship of the earth.

Unfortunately, my speech did not go over well. In 1982, earth care was not a popular subject among evangelical ministers. On the contrary, the environment was considered to be a liberal issue and thus highly suspect. During my presentation several men in the group were clearly unhappy with my remarks. After the session one of them walked up to me, visibly upset. He pointed his finger in my face and shouted in an angry voice, "Young man, God does not care about saving trees. God only cares about saving souls."

I thought about his comment for a moment and replied, "I think God cares about both. I think God cares about saving souls *and* saving trees." Unhappy with my response, he called me a "liberal tree hugger" and stomped away in anger. Even after all these years, I still vividly remember that painful experience. I was young, new in my vocation, and it deeply hurt to be rejected by my colleagues. However, decades later, I'm more convinced than ever that God cares about *both* saving souls *and* saving trees.

Going Public

Unfortunately, many churches in America overemphasize *personal* faith and underemphasize *public* faith. For example, these churches care deeply about personal salvation. More than anything, they want people to affirm faith in Jesus Christ. They also care deeply about personal moral behavior like drinking, cursing, and sexual purity. Both personal salvation and personal morality are important issues. However, these same churches (with a growing number of exceptions) care little about the environment, poverty, and peacemaking, even though these are major biblical concerns. When these churches do address social concerns, the only two issues that seem to matter are abortion and gay marriage. No doubt abortion and homosexuality are important social issues, but they are hardly exhaustive. God clearly cares about unborn children and sexual integrity, regardless of what side of these issues you come down on. But Scripture teaches us that God also cares passionately about poverty, the environment, race relations, peacemaking, health care, immigration, taxes, debt relief, just court systems, fair wages, prisons, and hunger. Since these issues matter to God, they should also matter to God's church.

Public Not Partisan

I am *not* advocating, however, that churches engage in partisan politics. Through the years many religious leaders and churches on both the right and the left have inappropriately identified themselves with either the Republican Party or the Democratic Party. But partisan politics, supporting a particular political candidate or party, has no place in the church of Jesus Christ, for at least five reasons.

First, partisan politics is illegal. As nonprofit organizations, churches are forbidden by law to participate directly in political campaigns. Second, partisan politics divides congregations, pitting Republicans, Democrats, and independents against one another. Third, partisan politics diverts the church from its primary mission. God did not create the church to be a political action committee. God commissioned the church for a sacred mission, one that transcends partisan politics. Fourth, partisan politics damages the integrity of the church. Historically, whenever the church lets itself be seduced by political power, the church always suffers, as it did in Nazi Germany and apartheid South Africa. When the church gets too close to the government, the church always loses. Finally, partisan politics politicizes God, reducing God to a political tool of the left or the right, which is completely unacceptable. People of faith must always remember that God is not a Republican or a Democrat or even an American. God is bigger than partisan politics.

Clearly the church has no business participating in partisan politics, left or right. However, that does not mean the church should avoid social issues like poverty, earth care, and peacemaking. Unfortunately, many churches in America have done precisely that. Other than fighting against abortion and gay marriage, they have abdicated social issues. They have focused primarily on private faith and ignored public faith.

Beyond Personal Religion

I do not disparage churches for emphasizing personal salvation and personal morality. These are important issues to me as well. For example, I want people to know Jesus. In fact, evangelism is a passion of mine, and my church reaches many unbelievers and longtime inactive Christians. And I want people to live pure and moral lives. But we must remember that God cares about many issues beyond personal salvation and personal morality like abortion and homosexuality. As Jim Wallis says so well, "God is personal but never private." In his book *God's Politics*, Wallis says:

> Restricting God to private space was the great heresy of the twentieth-century American evangelicalism. Denying the public God is a denial of biblical faith itself, a rejection of the prophets, the apostles, and Jesus himself. Exclusively private faith degenerates into a narrow religion, excessively preoccupied with individual and sexual morality while almost oblivious to the biblical demands for public justice.[1]

God cares about saving souls. But God also cares about saving trees, feeding hungry people, and establishing peace and justice in the world. Thankfully, a growing number of churches are beginning to understand this truth, including some conservative evangelical churches. May their tribe increase!

I recently heard an interesting story about Will Campbell, author of the profound book *Brother to a Dragonfly*. Campbell, a rebel Baptist preacher, got into trouble in the 1960s as an advocate for economic justice and racial equality in the South. Years ago, Will served in World War II and was assigned to a medical unit on an island. One evening, in the middle of the night, a sergeant woke Will up. They needed Will to help with an operation on a severely injured island boy. A crusty colonel from Atlanta performed the operation. Sadly the operation failed and the boy died.

After the operation the colonel asked the sergeant, "What happened to the boy?"

The sergeant told the colonel, "The child was a houseboy for a wealthy French planter. When the boy dropped an ashtray, the planter beat and kicked him without mercy."

The colonel, looking at the dead boy, said, "That's a hell of a price to pay for a goddamn ashtray."

After they delivered the dead boy to his family, the sergeant, a devout Christian, asked Will if he would go to the chapel and pray with him. Seeing a little boy beaten to death for dropping an ashtray would motivate almost anyone to pray, so Will went with the sergeant. When they arrived at the chapel, the sergeant prayed and prayed. But amazingly, he never prayed for the dead boy, or the boy's family, or for justice to be served to the man who murdered him. Instead, the sergeant only prayed for the colonel who had taken the Lord's name in vain. Indeed, the sergeant seemed profoundly distressed about the colonel's great sin.

It flabbergasted Will that the sergeant cared more about the colonel's cussing than he did about the tragic death of the houseboy or the gross injustice of the French planter. That experience has stuck with Will his entire life. It has helped him realize that when Christians focus too much on *private* faith—like cursing and sexual ethics—and neglect the larger issues of *public* faith—like compassion and justice—we've missed the point of religious faith.

A few months ago, while driving to a meeting, I noticed a little white church on the side of the road. A huge sign in front of the church said, "A Full Gospel Church." I thought to myself, *That's exactly what the world needs*. We need thousands of full-gospel churches that emphasize *personal* faith like accepting Jesus, being sexually pure, and using appropriate Christian language. But we also need full-gospel churches that emphasize *public* faith like caring for the environment, seeking peace, and fighting poverty. May God help your church and mine truly be "a full-gospel church."

❖ ❖ ❖

Bottom line: *God cares about personal salvation* and *social justice, and so should God's church.*

Note for Chapter 5

1. Jim Wallis, *God's Politics: Why the Right Gets It Wrong and the Left Doesn't Get It* (New York: HarperCollins, 2005), 35.

CHAPTER 6

⸎

BAD PEOPLE WILL
BE "LEFT BEHIND"
AND THEN FRY IN HELL

*About that day and hour no one knows, neither the angels of heaven,
nor the Son, but only the Father.*

—Jesus, in Matthew 24:36

When I was fifteen years old, I attended a youth lock-in at a conservative Southern church. After eating dinner and playing games, we had a Bible study on the second coming of Christ. The teacher talked about strange things, including the rapture, the antichrist, the seven-year tribulation, and Armageddon. Then we sang a song about the rapture called "I Wish We'd All Been Ready." The closing words of the song say, "There's no time to change your mind, the Son has come and you've been left behind." At that point they showed us a movie called *Like a Thief in the Night*, which depicted the rapture, the second coming of Christ, and the end of the world. It scared me half to death.

That youth lock-in was my first exposure to a theological view called "premillennial dispensationalism." This view is widely held among conservative and fundamentalist churches in the South. Made popular in the 1980s by a book called *The Late Great Planet Earth*, the same view is being promoted today by a series of wildly popular novels called Left Behind.

According to left-behind theology, Jesus will secretly come to earth and transport true believers to heaven. This is known as "the rapture." During the rapture people will literally be snatched up into heaven. That's the meaning behind those bumper stickers that say, "Warning: In Case of Rapture This Vehicle Will Be Unmanned." After the rapture those who are left behind will face seven years of tribulation. During these seven years of tribulation, the antichrist will inflict global warfare and horrible natural disasters upon the world. After seven years of tribulation, Christ will gloriously return and defeat the forces of evil at the great battle of Armageddon. That will be followed by Christ's one-thousand-year reign over the earth. After that the world will end, and eternity will begin. Although variations exist, in broad strokes that's the basic outline of left-behind rapture theology.

Although good people believe this theory, it's fraught with major problems. I'll quickly review four of them. For a more detailed critique, see Barbara R. Rossing's excellent book, *The Rapture Exposed: The Message of Hope in the Book of Revelation.*[1]

Biblical problems. The Bible does not support this elaborate, left-behind system of thought. For example, no passage in the Bible even uses the word *rapture.* Not one verse in the entire Bible talks about Christ's coming twice, once in secret to rapture his church and then a second time seven years later. The Bible teaches that Jesus will return once and once only. The only way to make this theory work is to take dozens of unrelated biblical passages, many of them obscure and most of them out of context, and piece them together into an elaborate system. Contrary to what this view claims, the Bible does not lay out a detailed master plan of the end of the world. Even the book of Revelation is not a road map to the future; it spoke to the people of its day. For example, it dealt with many issues of first-century Rome, including Emperor Nero and the persecution of the early Christians. In short, the entire left-behind rapture theory does great injustice to the Bible.

Historical problems. Left-behind rapture theology is a new invention in the church. This theory was first developed in 1830 by a man named John Darby. For over eighteen hundred years the church did not hold this view. Until then, the church simply affirmed that one day Jesus would return, judge the world, and usher in the final kingdom of God. For example, no rapture is mentioned in the two great historical affirmations of faith, the Apostles' Creed and the Nicene Creed. Left-behind theology is not the historical faith of the church.

Theological problems. Left-behind theology presents God as a vengeful, bloody, wrath-filled, violent deity. The God of left-behind theology doesn't remotely resemble Jesus' view of God as the loving heavenly Father who seeks to redeem the world. Left-behind theology gets God all wrong.

Social problems. For all practical purposes, left-behind rapture theology abandons the world that God has created and wants to renew. For example, people who hold this view often say that nuclear war is inevitable, the pursuit of peace is pointless, and environmental woes are unstoppable. As a result, there is no call for social justice, no concern about caring for the environment, and no effort to make peace among the nations. It's a recipe for social irresponsibility and even social disaster.

All You Need to Know
about the Second Coming of Christ

If left-behind theology gets it wrong, and it most certainly does, what *does* the Bible teach about the second coming of Christ? In a nutshell, the Bible teaches four truths about last things. First, Jesus will return. The Bible clearly affirms that one day Christ will return and end history. Second, we don't know the details. Therefore, we should not speculate about them. Third, we need to be ready. We prepare for the second coming by affirming faith in Jesus Christ. Fourth, we need to be working. Before Jesus returns, we are called to engage in God's work to share the gospel, meet human need, and seek justice for all people. Those four things are really all we need to know about the second coming of Christ.

Final Judgment

The Bible tells us that when Christ does return, he will judge all persons. As the Apostles' Creed affirms, Jesus "shall come to judge the quick and the dead." The "quick and the dead" simply means the living and the dead. Every person who ever lives will one day be judged by Christ. Thankfully, by the grace and mercy of God and the sacrifice of Jesus, Christian believers will be spared punishment. But what about nonbelievers? What happens to people who reject Christ? What happens to people who never seek God's mercy, who never spiritually prepare for death or the return of Christ? Christians hold three different theories on this subject. An overview of each theory follows.

Eternal punishment. This traditional view of hell says that people who reject God in life will be forever separated from God in eternity, with no hope of salvation. Some proponents of this view say that people in hell will be forever tormented with flames of fire. Others say we should not take that literally since hell is also described as a place of utter darkness. The point is, hell is a bad place, a place where God is not to be found, and a place where there is no hope.

Although some biblical passages support this view, it's fiercely debated. For example, many theologians and biblical scholars argue that if this position is true, God ultimately loses. If people are forever cut off from God, then God will eternally be sorrowful that many are forever alienated from God's love. Another problem with this view, according to its critics, is that being banished to an eternal hell is a highly disproportionate penalty. For example, if a person is caught stealing a twenty-dollar CD from Wal-Mart, the courts don't give them life in prison or the death penalty. That would be disproportionate punishment. That same thinking says that even if people live horrible lives for seventy or eighty years, it would not be just to punish them for all eternity. They argue that God would not punish people so disproportionately. In spite of these concerns, this traditional view of eternal punishment is held by many sincere and good Christian people, especially among conservative churches.

Possible redemption. This second view holds out hope that people, even after death, can be redeemed. People who affirm this position argue that there is no place, not even hell itself, that is cut off from God's grace, love, and mercy. This view holds out the hope of final salvation for all, a view known as universalism. Many people who hold this position do believe in hell. However, they view hell as redemptive punishment—punishment given not for vengeance but for purifying. For example, author Madeleine L'Engle once said: "I cannot believe that God wants punishment to go on interminably any more than does a loving parent. The entire purpose of loving punishment is to teach, and it lasts only as long as is needed for the lesson. And the lesson is always love."[2]

Advocates of this view sometimes argue that the phrase in the Apostles' Creed that says Jesus "descended into hell" was God's way to give people who have died another opportunity to say yes to God. They also point to several passages in the Bible that seem to hold out hope that, in the end, all persons will eventually come to God. For example, they believe that 1 Peter 3 and 4 suggest that after his death, Jesus went to hell to proclaim the gospel, giving nonbelievers a second chance. Although this position is certainly not clear-cut in the Bible, some support exists for this view. As a result, a good number of theologians and biblical scholars affirm this position.

Final annihilation. This view says that people who reject God will ultimately cease to be; they will be annihilated and exist no more. Instead of eternal punishment, their lives will be extinguished. Numerous passages in the Bible seem to support this view. Therefore a growing number of scholars, including conservative scholars, support this view of final annihilation. For an engaging and comprehensive view of all three of these positions, see *Razing Hell: Rethinking Everything You've Been Taught about God's Wrath and Judgment,* by Sharon L. Baker.

What happens to nonbelievers after death? What is their final destiny? Some say they will spend eternity in hell, forever separated from God. Others say they will have a second chance for redemption. Still others say they will finally cease to be: they will be annihilated. Which one is right? I'm happy to give you the definitive answer: we don't know! Good Christians disagree on this topic. In the end we simply have to trust God to do the right thing, whatever that is.

❊ ❊ ❊

Bottom line: *Left-behind rapture theology is neither a biblical nor a historical Christian belief and should be left behind by mainline and moderate evangelical Christians. The final destiny of non-believers is in God's hands, not ours, and God can be trusted to do what's right.*

Notes for Chapter 6

1. Barbara R. Rossing, *The Rapture Exposed: The Message of Hope in the Book of Revelation* (Boulder, CO: Westview Press, 2004).

2. Christopher W. Morgan and Robert A. Peterson, eds., *Hell under Fire: Modern Scholarship Reinvents Eternal Punishment* (Grand Rapids: Zondervan, 2004), 171.

CHAPTER 7

⬥⬥⬥

JEWS WON'T MAKE
IT TO HEAVEN

"I now realize how true it is that God does not show favoritism,
but accepts men from every nation who fear him and do what is right."
—Peter, in Acts 10:34–35, NIV

Several months ago an adult Sunday school class in my church asked me to visit. They wanted me to answer the question, Will Jews make it to heaven? When I arrived at the class, the leader immediately asked, "So, will Jews make it to heaven?" Before I could respond, another member of the class said, "And while you're at it, what about Muslims, Hindus, and Buddhists?"

Imagine for a moment a global village of one thousand people. Further imagine that these one thousand people represent, proportionally, all the religions of the world. If that were true, three hundred of the one thousand people would be Christians. Two hundred people in the village would have no religion at all. The other five hundred people in the village would be made up of non-Christian religions, including Muslims, Hindus, Buddhists, and Jews. In our imaginary village, 30 percent would be Christians, 20 percent would have no religion, and 50 percent would practice non-Christian religions. This raises the question for Christian believers, What about the 50 percent? What attitude should Christians have toward other religions? Let's explore three popular answers to that question.

All religions are the same. This view is popular among many folks, including a good number of Christians. This position says that in spite of apparent differences, all religions, in the end, are basically the same. The problem with this view is that it's inaccurate. All religions are *not* the same. Certainly similarities can be found. For example, most religions try to connect human beings with the sacred, most religions have sacred scriptures, and most religions teach compassion and ethical living. However, in spite of these similarities, vast differences exist between religions.

For example, take Christianity and Judaism. Christians have much in common with the Jewish faith. Christianity was born in Judaism and participated in Jewish faith for many decades. But in spite of their similarities, significant differences persist, primarily around the person of Jesus Christ. Jews teach that Jesus was a good man, a teacher, even a prophet, but no more. Christians teach that Jesus was the Messiah, the son of God, the second person of the Trinity. These are not minor differences! Christianity and Judaism are not the same.

The same dynamics are true with Islam. In spite of similarities, Christianity and Islam have major, irresolvable differences. The differences are even more pronounced with Buddhism and Hinduism. For example, the Buddhist religion doesn't believe in a personal God, and Hindus believe in many gods. So to say that all religions are the same is naive, inaccurate, and a disservice to the uniqueness of each faith. Since this first view is not helpful, let's look at a second option.

Other religions are false. This view says that all non-Christian religions are false religions and not of God. Therefore, people who practice these religions do not know God and have no hope of salvation in this life or the next. This view may sound harsh to you, but it's held by many good people. In fact, it's the view I was taught as a young Christian. I vividly remember a Sunday school class I attended when I was fifteen years old. A missionary from another country was speaking. He told us it was imperative that we send more missionaries around the world because people who did not accept Christ were lost and going to hell.

I asked the missionary, "What about people who've never heard of Christ?"

He said, "They will die, lost in their sins, and spend eternity in a devil's hell."

I said, "You're kidding!"

But he wasn't kidding. This view believes strongly that the only way to God is through Jesus.

Where does this belief come from? Proponents of this view say that it comes from the Bible. For example, Acts 4:12 says, "There is salvation in no one else [Jesus], for there is no other name under heaven given among mortals by which we must be saved." At first glance it seems clear-cut: if people don't go through Jesus, they don't get to God. However, from the beginning of Christianity, followers of Christ have debated how to interpret passages like this, which seem so exclusive of non-Christian religions. Some Christians interpret these passages as absolute, literal, doctrinal truth. Others interpret these passages not as absolute dogma but as poetic and devotional in nature. For example, in his book *The Heart of Christianity*, New Testament scholar Marcus Borg says:

To say "Jesus is the only way" is also the language of devotion. It is the language of gratitude and love. It is like language used by lovers, as when we say to our beloved, "You're the most beautiful person in the world." Literally? Most beautiful? Really? Such language is the poetry of devotion and the hyperbole of the heart. Poetry can express the truth of the heart, but it is not doctrine. . . . [He concludes,] We can sing our love songs to Jesus with wild abandon without needing to demean other religions.[1]

Although Borg's argument makes sense to many people, it does not convince all Christians. Many conservative believers hold strongly to the view that all non-Christian religions are false, and people who practice them have no hope of salvation. Thankfully, a third option exists.

Other religions are to be respected. In this third view other religions have insight and value and should be respected. People who hold this position believe people of other faiths are following God to the best of their knowledge. They understand that in many ways our religion is determined by geography. For example, if we lived in Saudi Arabia, it's extremely doubtful that we would be Christian. Instead, there's more than a 99 percent chance that we would be Muslim. This third view has a more accepting, positive, and respectful view of non-Christian religions than the second view. However, many people who hold this position still believe in the primacy of Jesus Christ. They believe that Jesus is the best picture we have of God. Therefore, they fully support evangelism and missions because they want all people of all nations and religions to know Jesus. However, this position does not believe that non-Christians have no hope of salvation. Ultimately, they leave the judgment of non-Christians to God.

The view that other religions are to be respected has biblical support. For example, in Acts 10 we are introduced to a character named Cornelius. Cornelius was not a Christian, nor was he a Jew. He later became a Christian believer, but as this passage begins, he was not. Cornelius was a Gentile, a pagan in the eyes of most Christians and Jews at that time. In many ways Cornelius's religion was similar to today's Muslims. He believed in one God, worshiped God, gave alms to the poor, prayed daily, and lived an ethical life. Although Cornelius was not a Christian or a Jew, the Bible says that his prayers and alms were pleasing to God. This is extremely important. Even though Cornelius was neither Christian nor Jew, his religious practices pleased God. In this story the apostle Peter—who believed all Gentiles were pagans, cut off from God, with no hope of salvation—learned otherwise. At the end of the story, Peter says to Cornelius, "I now realize . . . that God does not show favoritism but accepts men from every nation who fear him and do what is right" (Acts 10:34–35 NIV). This passage, along with others in the Bible, respects other religions and holds out hope that people who practice non-Christian faiths can know God, please God, and participate in God's kingdom.

I serve on the theology committee of the Board of Ordained Ministry for United Methodists in Tennessee. That means I interview ministerial candidates who want to become Methodist preachers. In a recent interview one of the candidates was asked, "In the end, will people of other religions be saved and go to heaven?" The candidate said, "I don't know, but I hope so." That, in a nutshell, describes this third position.

Good Christian people disagree on this complex and controversial issue. In the end we must trust God to do the right thing concerning non-Christian religions, whatever the right thing is. But it seems to me that this third position of respecting other religions, while at the same time affirming the uniqueness of Christ, comes closest to the spirit of Jesus.

I once heard a true story about a quiet suburban neighborhood in Pennsylvania. Almost all of the families in that community were Christians. However, one family in the neighborhood was Jewish. Christmas season was rapidly approaching, and the entire neighborhood sparkled with Christmas decorations. However, the decorations at the Jewish family's home looked different. Instead of Christmas trees and lights, the Jewish home featured a large illuminated menorah in their front window. A Jewish menorah represents the Jewish holiday of Hanukkah, which falls at about the same time as Christmas. In many ways the menorah, like the Star of David, is a universal symbol of Judaism.

A few days before Christmas, at five o'clock one morning, the Jewish family awoke to the sound of shattering glass. The family ran downstairs and saw that their front window had been broken. Their illuminated menorah lay on the floor, beaten to pieces. The attack was a horrible assault on this Jewish family and on their religion. The pain of the assault was compounded even more by the fact that their grandparents had died in the concentration camps of Nazi Germany during World War II. The husband immediately began to clean up the mess and had the window replaced. It took all morning to finish everything. During the day word spread throughout the neighborhood about what happened. Many neighbors came by and told this family how sorry they were that this awful thing had occurred in their neighborhood.

Later that afternoon the Jewish family left their home to visit relatives. They did not know that behind the scenes, their Christian neighbors were hard at work, trying to redeem this horrible event. That night, when the Jewish family returned from visiting their relatives, they were met by an extraordinary sight. On the front window of nearly every home in their neighborhood hung a large illuminated menorah.

❀ ❀ ❀

Bottom line: *The ultimate destiny of non-Christians is in God's hands, and God can be trusted to do what's right.*

Note for Chapter 7

1. Marcus Borg, *The Heart of Christianity: Rediscovering a Life of Faith* (New York: HarperCollins, 2004), 221–22.

CHAPTER 8

⚭

EVERYTHING IN
THE BIBLE SHOULD
BE TAKEN LITERALLY

O daughter Babylon, you devastator!
Happy shall they be who pay you back
what you have done to us!
Happy shall they be who take your little ones
and dash them against the rock!

—Psalm 137:8–9

Many centuries ago a bald holy man walked down a road on his way to the city. As he neared the city, he came upon a group of boys. When the boys saw his bald head, they began to tease him, saying, "Go away, Baldhead! Go away, Baldhead!" In anger the holy man called down God's curse upon the little boys. Immediately, two vicious bears emerged from the woods and mauled them. Unfazed by the screaming, violence, and blood from the bears' ripping the little boys' bodies apart, the holy man continued his journey into the city.

Where does that awful story come from? It comes from the story of the prophet Elisha in the Holy Bible (2 Kings 2:23–25). And there are plenty more biblical texts just like it, including the vengeful passage listed above from Psalm 137. In this text the psalmist, full of hatred for the Babylonians, wants to murder Babylonian infants by smashing their little bodies against the rocks.

Somewhere along the way, Christian believers must answer a crucial question about these kinds of troubling texts, which are so prevalent in the Bible. Are such passages meant to be taken literally? Does God really send bears from the woods to rip apart little boys for teasing a prophet? Or was this a campfire story the ancient Israelites told their children and grandchildren to engender respect for the holy prophets of Israel? How you answer that question will have a huge impact on how you understand Christian faith. Ultimately it will determine if you fall into the literalist, fundamentalist camp of Christianity or the mainline and moderate camp.

People hold one of three positions about biblical inspiration. People believe that the Bible is either (1) all human, (2) all divine, or (3) both human and divine. Let's review all three.

The Bible is all human. This position says the Bible is inspired, but no more so than Shakespeare or any other great work of literature. However, this is not a viable option for Christian believers who consider the Bible to be "the Word of God for the people of God." From the very beginning, Christians have affirmed that the Bible is "Holy Scripture." Although Christians hold differing views of biblical inspiration, as we'll see below, virtually all Christian believers and churches affirm that the Bible is divinely inspired. As a result, Christians hold the Bible in high esteem, turning to it for both doctrinal beliefs and behavioral guidance. Therefore, for the vast majority of Christians, an all-human Bible is not an acceptable option.

The Bible is all divine. This position says that everything in the Bible is literal, including all historic, geographical, and scientific details. Although this view is held by fundamentalist churches, it's not the historic Christian position. In fact, this view of the Bible, called "biblical inerrancy," is quite new in Christian history. It first appeared in the early 1900s in reaction to modern science (especially the theory of evolution) and modern biblical scholarship (called "the historical-critical method"). Conservative believers felt threatened by these modern views, so they adopted the concept of an "inerrant and infallible" Bible that could not be questioned by modern science or scholarship. Unfortunately, this view of Scripture is overwhelmingly problematic. For example, if everything in the Bible is literal, then —

- The earth is flat.
- Creation took place six thousand years ago.
- The world was created in six, twenty-four-hour days.
- Women are the property of men.
- Slavery is approved by God.
- Polygamy is approved by God.
- In order to win a bet with the devil, God let Satan kill all ten of Job's children.
- God throws raging, jealous, violent fits, killing thousands in the process.
- Eating shellfish is an abomination to God.
- Wearing blended garments (like cotton/polyester) enrages God.
- Menstruating women and handicapped men are not allowed in public worship.
- God's preferred system of government is a monarchy.
- All governments, even highly oppressive ones, are established by God.

- God approves of genocide and commanded people to practice it.
- Woman are to be silent in church.
- Women are to wear veils in church.
- People who commit adultery should be stoned to death.
- The penalty for working on the Sabbath is execution.
- Sassy teenagers are to be executed.

The above examples are just a few of the massive problems that come with biblical inerrancy. For example, if the Bible is all divine, how do you explain its inconsistencies? In the book of Matthew, we are told that Judas, the disciple who betrayed Jesus, hanged himself. However, in the book of Acts, we are told that Judas fell down in a field and died from massive internal rupturing of his organs. Both stories can't be true. So why do we have two conflicting stories in Scripture about the death of Judas? The answer is simple. When the Bible was written—many decades after the original events occurred—two different stories were circulating about Judas's death. The writer of Matthew picked up one story, and the writer of Acts picked up the other. If space permitted, hundreds of examples of inconsistencies in the Bible could be given, including conflicting accounts of the birth and resurrection of Christ.

Another example of the problems that come with biblical literalism can be found in the familiar story of Noah and the ark in Genesis 6–8. Although many people believe that the Noah story literally happened, a lot of sincere and thoughtful Christians are reluctant, for several reasons, to affirm a literal reading of the text. First, no scientific evidence exists to suggest that the earth ever experienced a worldwide flood. Major floods have occurred locally and regionally, but it's doubtful that the entire earth ever flooded. Also, how is it possible that every species on the planet was placed into one boat, even a big one? From a scientific analysis, the story has overwhelming problems. Second, the Genesis flood story is extremely similar to an ancient Babylonian myth that predates the Bible. Even a casual reading of the two stories leads to the likely conclusion that the Israelites borrowed the ancient story, adapted it, and retold it according to their purposes. Finally, significant theological challenges exist with the passage. If the Noah story literally happened, then God purposely annihilated every living creature on the earth in a worldwide genocidal flood. This image of God is hard to reconcile with Jesus' teachings that God is like a heavenly Father who deeply loves his children, even sinful ones like the prodigal son. Valuable theological lessons can be found in the story of Noah, including the fact that God takes sin seriously, and God expects us, like Noah, to live righteous and faithful lives in a pagan culture. But one can affirm these theological truths without believing in a literal, worldwide, genocidal flood.

Many years ago I had a conversation about biblical literalism with an extremely conservative pastor. We were talking about the Old Testament stories of David killing his archenemies, the Philistines. Several of those stories claim that David singlehandedly killed hundreds of Philistines at a time. I said to this pastor, "What if the biblical writers exaggerated the number of Philistines that David killed in any given battle? What if he only killed thirty instead of three hundred? Would that matter?" The pastor replied, "If that were true, I would have to quit the ministry and renounce my faith. If I can't believe everything in the Bible, then I can't believe anything in the Bible." Sadly, this kind of radical literalism is extremely damaging to the Christian faith. It forces people to take an all-or-nothing approach to Scripture, a totally unnecessary choice that the Bible does not require.

For these and many other reasons, the vast majority of Christian believers do not affirm biblical inerrancy. And they don't need to affirm or accept it. Only a small percentage of Christians advocate this position. The Bible itself never claims to be inerrant; it claims only to be inspired. Biblical inerrancy has never been the historic position of the church. In fact, the church existed for nineteen centuries *without* this view. Belief in biblical inerrancy is not necessary for Christians and is, in fact, detrimental to authentic faith. Telling people they must believe something that intellectual and theological integrity cannot authentically accept only hurts the Christian cause. Thankfully, a third and far more promising position exists concerning biblical inspiration.

The Bible is both human and divine. This is the classic position of the church, held by virtually all mainline and moderate denominations. This view states that the Bible was inspired by God. People who hold this position affirm, along with the Bible, that "all Scripture is God-breathed and is useful for teaching, rebuking, correcting and training in righteousness" (2 Tim. 3:16 NIV). The Christian church has always affirmed that God inspired the Bible, that Holy Scripture has a divine element. But the church also affirms that the Bible is a *human* document. People, not God, wrote the Bible. And they wrote it according to the worldview of their time, which was a prescientific world. For example, the biblical writers believed that the world was flat and that mental illness was caused by demons. Those kinds of prescientific views are reflected throughout the Bible.

A concrete example of human involvement in the Bible is found in Luke 1. Luke begins his Gospel by writing, "Therefore, since I have carefully investigated everything from the beginning, it seemed good also to me to write an orderly account" (1:3 NIV). We clearly see human involvement here. Luke did his homework. He researched his subject well and eventually wrote the Gospel of Luke and the book of Acts. Although God inspired Luke's writing, Luke was fully involved in the process. In short, Luke's Gospel is the product of divine inspiration as well as human insight and human limitations.

Clearly Christians do not have to interpret everything in the Bible literally. In fact, since some passages of Scripture express pre-Christian and even sub-Christian views of God, Christians *should* not interpret everything literally. However, that does *not* mean the Bible is not true. For example, take the first book of the Bible. Genesis is full of many great truths: God created the world, human beings are created in God's image, human sin is real, and God dearly loves all creation. However, a person can believe these great truths without believing that the earth is flat, that the world is only six thousand years old, that serpents talk to people, or that Noah literally placed two representatives of every living creature on earth into one boat.

I love the Bible. My life has been transformed by the message of the Bible. I believe that the Bible is true and trustworthy and reliable. I affirm the great truths of the Bible. For example, I believe God created the world. I believe God called Abraham and Sarah to give birth to a nation through whom God blessed the world. I believe the Ten Commandments and the prophet's demands for justice. I believe the Great Commandment, the Great Commission, and the Golden Rule. And most important, I believe, as the Bible teaches, in the life, death, and bodily resurrection of Jesus Christ. However, like most Christians through most of Christian history, I do not believe that everything in the Bible has to be understood literally.

Christians must always remember that we worship God, not the Bible. The Bible *points* us to God, but the Bible is *not* God. Many years ago John the Baptist came upon the scene, preparing the way for Jesus. When people went to hear John preach, they asked him, "Are you the Messiah?"

John said, "No, I am not the Messiah, but I bear witness to the Messiah." The same is true for the Bible. The Bible is not God, but the Bible bears witness to God. Therefore, Holy Scripture is central to our faith.

❊ ❊ ❊

Bottom line: *Although we must always take the Bible seriously, we don't always have to take it literally.*

CHAPTER 9

⚭

GOD LOVES STRAIGHT PEOPLE BUT NOT GAY PEOPLE

For now we see in a mirror, dimly.

—Paul, in 1 Corinthians 13:12

You may be familiar with a minister named Fred Phelps. He's the angry preacher who travels around the country holding a sign that says, "God Hates Fags." Although there's much I don't know about God, I do know that God does *not* hate homosexuals.

American churches are not of one mind concerning homosexuality. Good Christian people vigorously disagree over this volatile subject. In spite of decades of spirited debate, mainline and moderate churches have not yet resolved this issue. Obviously, I'm not going to resolve it in this short chapter. However, homosexuality is a huge topic in today's church and needs to be addressed. Although an oversimplification, Christians hold three major views concerning homosexuality. These three views are represented by the Christian right, the Christian left, and the Christian center. Let's review all three.

The Christian right: nonwelcoming and nonaffirming. The first major position on homosexuality can often be found among the Christian right. Churches that hold this position can be summarized as *nonwelcoming and nonaffirming.* Although these churches might say homosexuals are welcome, for all practical purposes, practicing homosexuals are not welcome in their church. Not only are these churches nonwelcoming; they are also nonaffirming. They do not affirm or accept homosexual behavior of any kind. Instead, they harshly condemn it. They base their position on several biblical passages, which they believe unequivocally condemn homosexual behavior.

Although this view tries to be faithful to the Bible and historical teachings of the church concerning homosexuality, it has serious weaknesses. First, it singles out homosexuality as a far-worse sin than other sins. For example, the same biblical passages that condemn homosexual acts also condemn greed, lust, gossip, envy, gluttony, pride, and disrespect toward parents. Churches that hold this nonwelcoming and nonaffirming view tend to put an unwritten sign on their front door that warns, NO HOMOSEXUALS ALLOWED. But if they want to be consistent with the Bible, they would also need to put up a sign that says, "No greedy people allowed, no gluttons allowed, no gossips allowed, no arrogant people allowed, no lustful people allowed, and no envious persons allowed." Of course, if you did that, soon no church members would remain. If all sinners were outlawed from church, our pews—and our pulpits—would be empty. So a major weakness of this view is that it unfairly lifts up homosexuality as a worse sin than all other sins.

A second weakness of this position is that it deeply wounds homosexuals and their loved ones. Sadly, people who hold this view are often (but not always) mean-spirited about it, and sometimes they say horrible things about gay people. For example, a minister in my community recently said in a sermon, "Homosexuals will not be allowed into heaven." This harsh and even hateful judgment profoundly hurts homosexual persons and pushes them away from God and God's church.

I once heard about a minister who officiated at a funeral for a man who died of AIDS. Several other pastors in town refused to handle the funeral because the man was gay and because those attending the funeral would also be gay. About thirty homosexual men showed up for the graveside funeral. The minister conducted the service the best he could. He then said the closing prayer and gave the blessing, but the men didn't budge. He motioned them to leave, but they wouldn't.

Finally he said, "Is there anything more I can do for you?"

One of them said, "Yeah, they usually read the Twenty-third Psalm at these things. Would you mind reading it?"

He did.

Then someone said, "Isn't there something in the Bible about nothing separating us from God's love? Can you read that?"

He turned to Romans 8 and read the text.

Then one of the men said, "Could you read that passage about God raising us up on eagle's wings?"

And he turned to Isaiah 40 and read. This went on and on.

I wept as I listened to that story. These men desperately wanted to hear the Word of God, to know God's love, and to have spiritual connections in their lives; they were starving for God. Many of them had been raised and nurtured in God's church and still loved God. However, because of their sexual orientation, people told them they were deviant, hated by God, and unwanted at church.

Harsh judgment from Christians had pushed them away from God and church. In short, a nonwelcoming position on homosexuality is not an authentic Christian option.

The Christian left: welcoming and affirming. The second major position concerning homosexuality can often be found among the Christian left. This position can be summarized as *welcoming and affirming.* This position fully welcomes gays and lesbians into the church. However, they don't just welcome gays, they also affirm homosexual relationships. They point out that the Bible speaks very little about homosexuality. In fact, the entire Bible has only about seven references to homosexuality. Jesus never mentioned it once. On the other hand, they argue, the Bible is full of passages about God's love, grace, and acceptance. They also argue that the Bible knows nothing of homosexual orientation. In ancient days people just assumed that folks who practiced homosexuality were heterosexuals engaging in same sex behavior.

People who choose the welcoming and affirming position claim that homosexuals do not choose their sexual preference. They argue that it's just the way they are, the way God created them. They point to a growing number of scientific studies that suggest a strong link between homosexuality, genetics, and hormones. They also say the Bible knows nothing of loving, monogamous gay relationships. Finally, they argue that the biblical passages about homosexuality need to be understood in their specific historical context. This view claims that just as the church has changed its position through the years on slavery and women's rights, we need to do the same concerning homosexuality. They make a passionate case that the church not only needs to welcome gays into the church but that the church also needs to affirm loving monogamous gay relationships.

Although this position affirms God's love, grace, and acceptance for all persons, it has plenty of critics. For example, people who reject this view claim that it dismisses two thousand years of biblical and historical tradition concerning homosexuality. They also say that by pushing the church to adopt this view, the Christian left is helping create significant conflict in every major mainline denomination in the United States.

The Christian center: welcoming but nonaffirming. The third major position concerning homosexuality, often found in the Christian center, can be summarized as *welcoming but nonaffirming.* This position is fully welcoming: all persons, including gays, are absolutely welcome into the church of Jesus Christ. However, this position is nonaffirming: it is not yet ready to affirm homosexual behavior. This third position is where my denomination, the United Methodist Church, currently stands. Although we continue to discuss and debate this topic, for now we fall into this third camp. Of course, not all United Methodists affirm position 3. A strong minority in the UMC is pushing the church to adopt position number 2, welcoming and affirming. But for the present moment the majority of United Methodists affirm position 3, welcoming yet nonaffirming. This view is affirmed in *The Book of Discipline of the United Methodist Church.* For example, the Discipline affirms that homosexual persons have sacred worth, are welcome at our churches, and deserve full human and civil rights. However, the United Methodist Church does not affirm homosexual behavior, will not ordain practicing homosexual clergy, and will not celebrate homosexual unions.

Although this position tries to balance God's love, grace, and acceptance with the biblical and historical teachings of the church concerning homosexuality, it also has limitations. For example, those on the right feel that it's overly welcoming. They believe that homosexual persons should repent of their lifestyle before they are welcomed into Christ's church. However, those on the left believe that this position is not welcoming enough: if we are truly to welcome gays, they argue, then we need *completely* to welcome them by affirming loving, monogamous, same-sex relationships, by performing gay marriages, and by ordaining gay clergy. This view complains that we are inconsistent. We say gays are welcome, and we say we that we support gay rights, but we don't go all the way. So both the left and the right are disappointed by this policy.

Years ago, when I was a PhD student at Vanderbilt University, my bishop sent me to a small, struggling, Methodist church. At the time the church was seriously grappling with this issue of homosexuality. To make a long story short, the previous pastor had been pushing hard for the congregation to change their position on homosexuality. Not only did he want them to be a welcoming church, which they were, but he also wanted them to be an affirming church, which they were not. His aggressive push to approve homosexual behavior created massive conflict in the church. By the time I arrived, over half the membership had already left, and the other half were barely speaking to one another.

To appreciate this story, you need to know that the congregation included an openly gay couple, two men I'll call John and Mike. You also need to know that John and Mike were warmly welcomed and beloved members of that church. During my first few months on the job, I decided to visit in the home of every family in the congregation. Since the church was engaged in serious conflict over the gay issue, the subject came up in every one of my home visits. A few families told me that homosexual relationships were fine with them. On the other hand, several other families told me they did not approve of homosexual relationships. The vast majority of families said something like this: "We're not sure what to think about homosexuality, but we're not quite ready to affirm it." Like most mainline congregations, people in that church expressed ambivalence about homosexual relationships. But when it came to the gay couple in the congregation, John and Mike, there was absolutely no disagreement and no ambiguity. Every family in that church said, in so many words, "John and Mike are members of our church family. We love them dearly. They are welcome in this place."

Fully welcoming but not fully affirming, imperfect as it is, describes many if not most mainline and moderate Christians. We're still talking about it and debating it. We're still studying it and praying about it. So maybe one day our position will change. But for now this is where most of us stand.

❖ ❖ ❖

Bottom line: *All persons, including homosexual persons, are welcome in God's church. Beyond that, however, mainline and moderate churches are not of one mind on this issue. For now, "welcoming but not affirming" best describes most mainline churches, and the discussion goes on.*

CHAPTER 10

⸙

IT'S OK FOR CHRISTIANS TO BE JUDGMENTAL AND OBNOXIOUS

Do not judge, so that you may not be judged.

—Jesus, in Matthew 7:1

I vividly remember when karaoke machines first came out. I remember because a karaoke machine created trouble for me and my church. When the machines first hit the market, a member of my congregation named James purchased one. James, one of our most dedicated members, served as a deacon, taught a large Sunday school class, and sang in the choir. James had a beautiful tenor voice. One Sunday night James brought his karaoke machine to a churchwide fellowship, and everyone had a blast singing with it. James even convinced me to sing a Neil Diamond song with the machine, much to the delight of our members. James became a bit of a celebrity in our town, singing at parties and other events on his karaoke machine. Before long James was singing at a local bar on Friday nights. He didn't drink; he just sang. The people at the bar enjoyed James's singing so much that he became a permanent fixture on Friday nights.

Meeting with the Pharisees

Several months later a couple from my congregation came to see me. Although they attended every Sunday and gave lots of money, I've never known more judgmental people. Their self-righteous, holier-than-thou attitude was extremely obnoxious. Jesus himself would not have been good enough for them. After closing my office door, they said, "Pastor, we have a problem in this church that you need to take care of." At that point, they began to complain about James's singing at the bar. They said it was sinful, a poor witness, and was hurting the reputation of our church.

"What do you want me to do about it?" I asked them.

They said, "We want you to remove James from the deacon board, take away his Sunday school class, and ban him from singing in the choir. In fact, we think he should be kicked out of the church altogether."

I knew it would be difficult if not impossible to satisfy this self-righteous and judgmental couple. However, I tried to reason with them. I said, "I'm not sure if James's behavior is sinful or not. He's not drinking at the bar; he's only singing. And while we may think that Christians shouldn't hang out at bars, we need to remember that Jesus used to hang out with sinners, tax collectors, and even prostitutes. I'm not convinced that his singing at the bar is a sin."

They shot back, "Of course it's a sin! How could it not be?"

After thirty minutes of this kind of dialogue, I knew I could not satisfy them. So I gulped hard and said, "Even if it is sinful, I'm not going to remove James from the deacon board, take away his Sunday school class, or ban him from the choir. And I'm sure not going to kick him out of the church. If I kicked out every sinner in this church, we wouldn't have any deacons left, we wouldn't have any Sunday school teachers left, and we wouldn't have any choir members left. In fact, if we kicked out all the sinners in this church, we wouldn't have any members left at all, including me. I'm sorry, but I cannot do what you are asking."

As I expected, they were not happy with my response. "Pastor," they said, "if you don't do this, we will leave the church."

I replied, "I hope you won't leave. You are important people in this church, and we don't want to lose you. But I am not going to kick James out of the church for singing at a bar."

In the end we both kept our word. I didn't kick James out, and they left the church.

Unfortunately, some Christians have a self-righteous, judgmental spirit. Sadly, that kind of mean-spirited religion hurts the reputation of Christianity and is the complete opposite of the grace-filled spirit of Jesus Christ.

Getting the Ballast Right

Judgmental Christianity reminds me of a story that has troubled me ever since I heard it. Many years ago a ship sank off the coast of Nova Scotia during a winter storm. Many people perished, including the captain. The crew gathered seventy of the passengers, including women and children, and put them into a huge, open rowboat. However, the weather got rough, and the crew thought the boat was overcrowded. In an effort to get the ballast right, they picked up people and tossed them into the sea. Then the boat started leaking. Throughout the night, as the boat sank lower, more people were thrown off the boat to drown in the frigid waters. The next morning the crew arrived on shore with only nine people on board.

Tragically, judgmental churches often act like that. They want to get the ballast just right, so they throw out the sinners. Most churches don't do that formally, although some do. Most do it informally: they just let people know they are not welcome. But one way or another, they get rid of them. Like the sailors in the above story, they throw out the sinners. Here are divorced persons: let's throw them out. Here are alcoholics and drug addicts: let's throw them out. Here's an unwed mother: let's throw her out. Here's a liberal: let's throw him out. Here's a woman minister: let's throw her out. Here's a person who believes in evolution: let's throw her out. Here's a homosexual: let's throw him out.

About ten years ago a vibrant growing church in the South called a new pastor. The pastor decided his congregation needed purifying. He discovered that a member of his church owned a convenience store and sold beer, so the pastor and deacons kicked him out. Then they kicked out a Sunday school teacher who questioned biblical inerrancy. Next they kicked out a college student for getting pregnant out of wedlock. They followed that by kicking out a couple who questioned the right of the pastor to rule like a dictator. This went on and on. Within a year the church dropped from five hundred in worship to about fifty. The following year they went belly-up and closed the church. Such is the *destructive power of judgmental religion.*

Of course, this kind of judgmental religion is not new. In Jesus' day a group of self-righteous religious leaders constantly dogged Jesus. They were holier-than-thou and extremely judgmental. They believed they had all the right answers, and they condemned everyone who didn't agree with them. They were also the only people whom Jesus didn't get along with. In fact, Jesus constantly challenged their arrogant, judgmental spirit. He taught his followers to avoid their kind of self-righteous religion and leave judgment to God.

Several years ago my good friend temporarily quit going to church. He was going through a difficult divorce, and for a while he stopped attending worship. Soon thereafter, a judgmental Christian coworker began hounding him to attend her church. She had no concern for his personal struggles; she just knew he was going to hell if he didn't go to church. Although she was obnoxious, he tried for many months to be nice to her. Finally she wore him down.

One day she asked my friend, "Don't you want to go to heaven?"

In weary exasperation he responded, "Not if it's full of people like you."

✿ ✿ ✿

Bottom line: *True Christians leave judgment to God.*

PART 2

∽◌∽

TEN THINGS CHRISTIANS
DO NEED TO BELIEVE

So far we've reviewed ten things Christians *don't* need to believe. But that raises the question, what *do* Christians need to believe? The short answer is *Jesus*. We can discard many religious beliefs and still be Christians. However, we cannot discard Jesus.

When I served as a pastor in Hawaii, a Jewish man regularly attended my church. One day he said, "Pastor, I enjoy coming to your church. But is all that talk about Jesus really necessary?"

"Well, we are a Christian church," I replied, "and Jesus sort of goes with the territory."

We both laughed, and he said, "I guess you have a point there."

The nonnegotiable item in Christianity is Jesus Christ. Take Jesus out of the church, and you might have an impressive religious organization, a nice building, and noble ethical teachings, but you won't have Christianity.

So what's the least a person can believe and still be a Christian? The answer is *Jesus*.

In the pages that follow, we'll look at ten important Christian beliefs. However, I want to state clearly that the following chapters do not provide a comprehensive overview of Christian doctrines. *What's the Least I Can Believe and Still Be a Christian?* is not a systematic theology textbook. Instead, the following chapters illustrate that the life, death, and resurrection of Jesus Christ provide answers to some of life's most important questions:

- Who Is Jesus?
- What Matters Most?
- Am I Accepted?
- Where Is God?
- What Brings Fulfillment?
- What about Suffering?
- Is There Hope?
- Is the Church Still Relevant?
- Who Is the Holy Spirit?
- What Is God's Dream for the World?

To these significant questions let us now turn.

CHAPTER 11

⟨∽⟩

JESUS' IDENTITY

Who Is Jesus?

But who do you say that I am?

—Jesus, in Matthew 16:15

You don't expect a crude comedy about NASCAR racing starring Will Ferrell to raise issues about the identity of Jesus Christ. However, *Talladega Nights: The Ballad of Ricky Bobby* does exactly that. In the funniest scene of the movie, NASCAR racer Ricky Bobby, along with his family and best friend Cal, gather for a dinner of Domino's Pizza, KFC, and Taco Bell. Before they eat, Ricky offers grace.

He begins his prayer, "Dear Lord Baby Jesus." He then proceeds to thank baby Jesus for various blessings, including his "red-hot smoking wife, Carley." As he prays, he continues to repeat the phrase, "Dear Lord Baby Jesus."

Carley interrupts him and says, "You know, Sweetie, Jesus did grow up. You don't always have to call him baby."

Ricky Bobby replies, "I like the Christmas Jesus best, and I'm saying grace. When you say grace, you can say it to grown-up Jesus, or teenage Jesus, or bearded Jesus, or whoever you want."

Ricky Bobby continues his prayer, "Dear tiny Jesus, in your golden fleece diapers, with your tiny balled-up fists."

His father-in-law angrily interrupts, "He was a man. He had a beard!"

Ricky Bobby snaps back, "Listen, I'm saying grace, and I like the Christmas version best!"

Ignoring the conflict between the two men, Ricky Bobby's best friend Cal says, "I like to picture Jesus in a tuxedo T-shirt. It says like, I want to be formal, but I'm here to party too."

One of Ricky Bobby's sons says, "I like to picture Jesus as a Ninja, fighting off the evil samurai."

Cal then adds, "I like to think of Jesus with giant eagle wings and singing lead vocals for Lynyrd Skynyrd with an angel band."

Ricky Bobby returns to his prayer, saying, "Dear eight-pound, six-ounce, newborn infant Jesus, who doesn't even know a word yet — little infant, so cuddly but still omnipotent." He then thanks baby Jesus for all his NASCAR victories and the millions in prize money he has won. He concludes grace by saying, "Thank you for all your power and grace, dear Baby God. Amen."

Immediately after the prayer, Cal says, "That was a hell of a grace, man! You nailed that like a split hog!"

Count on Hollywood to raise important religious issues in such an irreverent yet hilarious way. That scene in *Talladega Nights*, irreverent as it is, raises major theological questions. Who is Jesus? Which version of Jesus is accurate? It's imperative that every person have a clear understanding of the identity of Jesus, for much is at stake.

Who Is This Man?

From the first century until today, speculation and debate have swirled around Jesus of Nazareth. People hold divergent and conflicting views about his identity. That was certainly true in Jesus' day. For example, John 7 tells a story about Jesus going to Jerusalem for a religious festival. By then Jesus has become quite a celebrity. The whole city is abuzz about this amazing miracle worker and teacher from Nazareth. However, no consensus has emerged concerning his identity.

Some people at the festival say, "He is a good man" (v. 12).

Others say, "No, he is deceiving the crowd" (v. 12).

Still others think Jesus is an insightful teacher. They say, "How does this man have such learning, when he has never been taught?" (v. 15).

A few believe Jesus is deranged. They say to him, "You have a demon!" (v. 20).

Others ask, "Can it be that . . . this is the Messiah?" (v. 26).

Electricity fills the air. People want to know: Who is this Jesus? Is he a good man, a deceitful threat, a wise teacher, a deranged lunatic—or is he perhaps the long-awaited Messiah?

This story from John's Gospel reminds me of an old Christian ballad called "Outlaw." The song, written by Larry Norman, offered five possible explanations of Jesus' identity. According to the ballad, some people in Jesus' day said he was an *outlaw* who roamed the land with his twelve partners in crime. Others said he was a *poet* who mesmerized the crowds with strange parables. Some claimed he was a *politician*, seeking a following for political gain. Many believed he was a *sorcerer*, performing magical feats that amazed people. However, some confessed that he was the *Son of God*, who came to serve and to save.

"Who Do You Say That I Am?"

The question of Jesus' identity is vividly raised in Matthew 16. In this story Jesus asks his disciples, "Who do people say that the Son of Man is?" (v. 13). After the disciples answer his question, Jesus asks them a second, more-important question. It's perhaps the most important question Jesus ever asks: "Who do *you* say that I am?" (v. 15, with added emphasis). In short, Jesus asks his disciples to make a verdict about his identity. For Christian believers the most important question in life is not, What career should I choose? Or, Whom should I marry? Or, Am I financially secure? Instead, the most important question in life is, Who is Jesus Christ to me?

When Jesus asks his disciples, "Who do you say that I am?" Peter responds, "You are the Christ, the Son of the living God" (Matt. 16:16 NIV). Peter's confession of faith is one of the most important christological affirmations ever made. Entire books have been written about this remarkable affirmation of faith, so I can only scratch the surface of Peter's comment. But in a nutshell Peter claims that Jesus is far more than a good man, a wise teacher, or even a prophet of God. Instead, Peter's confession is a profound affirmation of the divinity of Jesus—an affirmation that Christians have made ever since. When we confess Jesus as "Christ" (literally, the "Messiah"), we affirm that Jesus is the Savior of humanity, liberating us from sin, death, and hopelessness. When we confess Jesus as "the Son of the living God," we affirm that Jesus is uniquely related to God, fully reveals the nature of God, and connects us to God in a way no other person can. Therefore, when we, like Peter, affirm that Jesus is "the Christ, the Son of the living God," we acknowledge that Jesus is worthy of our highest praise and ultimate loyalty.

Making a Verdict about Jesus

At some point in life, every person needs to grapple with the question of Jesus' identity. We cannot defer the question to our parents, our preacher, or our church. Ultimately every person must answer Jesus' question: "Who do you say that I am?"

I answered that question many years ago. At the time I was a young, mixed-up, and troubled teenager. I didn't understand everything about Jesus then and still don't. However, I knew enough about Jesus to know that I desperately needed him in my life. So on a Sunday morning in a conservative Baptist church in Muskogee, Oklahoma, I affirmed my faith in Jesus Christ. The next Sunday morning I was baptized. It's the most important thing I've ever done—or ever will do—in my entire life.

Along with the apostle Peter, I believe Jesus is "the Christ, the Son of the living God." I place my faith and trust in Jesus. I accept his love, grace, and forgiveness. And I try to follow him as my Lord. I still have plenty of questions about Jesus. And I've had my share of doubts about him. However, Jesus has transformed my life and continues to transform it. Jesus gives my life meaning, direction, and purpose. Jesus gives me courage and strength for living. Jesus gives me hope for life and hope even for death. And as you will see in the following chapters, Jesus provides answers to my deepest questions. My faith in Jesus Christ is the most important part of my life. I hope the same is true for you. For further information about what it means to be a Christian believer and how to become one, please see chapter 21, "A Final Question: Do Mainline Christians Believe in Getting Saved?"

During my college years an acquaintance named Blake Greenway wrote a song about Jesus called, "If He Was Just a Man." The words go like this:

> I've heard his name most all my life.
> They tell me he once healed a blind man's eyes.
> They tell me he walked on the sea.
> They tell me he gave his own life for me.
>
> But if I really told the truth,
> I'd say sometimes I've doubted just like you.
> But there's one thing I go back to.
> There's one question I'd like to ask you.
> If he was just a man,
> There is one thing I cannot understand.
> How could he change my life so,
> If he was just a man?[1]

❀ ❀ ❀

Bottom line: *Jesus "the Christ, the Son of the living God," is the heart of Christianity.*

Note for Chapter 11

1. Lyrics quoted from "If He Was Just a Man," by Blake Greenway. Printed with permission of Blake Greenway.

CHAPTER 12

⁘

JESUS' PRIORITY

What Matters Most?

Of all the commandments, which is the most important?
                                    —a teacher of the law, in Mark 12:28 NIV

Steve and Lisa met and fell in love while earning their MBAs at a leading university. Young, sharp, and highly motivated, they shared a common goal to succeed in business, make a lot of money, and live the American dream. Immediately after receiving their MBA degrees, Steve and Lisa married. Soon thereafter they accepted business positions in a large city. A decade later found them earning huge incomes in major-league, high-finance corporations. Although their jobs routinely demanded sixty to eighty hours of work per week, the money was great, and they loved spending it. They bought a large house in a fashionable part of the city. Between the two of them, they owned four cars. They bought a cabin in the mountains about an hour outside the city. They even purchased a boat. Their entire lives focused on career success, money, and the stuff money could buy.

Steve and Lisa were now pushing forty years of age. With her biological clock ticking louder every year, Lisa wanted a child. About a year later they had a son, whom they named Nathan. Steve and Lisa had it all—youth, success, money, and now a beautiful child. But things were not right in their souls. Since both of them worked an enormous number of hours, Nathan stayed in day care all day, and a nanny took care of him most evenings. Steve and Lisa rarely spent time together and had minimal contact with their baby. And because of their busy schedules, they had virtually no time for friends, community affairs, or church. By the time Nathan was a year old, Steve and Lisa hit a crisis point. They asked themselves, "Is this all there is to life? Do we really want to put in endless hours at work in order to make more money and buy more stuff?"

Eventually Steve and Lisa realized that climbing the corporate ladder of success, making boatloads of money, and buying lots of stuff was not a big-enough life. So they made a life-changing decision. On the same day they both resigned their jobs. Steve took a forty-hour-a-week job managing a small business that paid less than half of his corporate salary. Lisa took a part-time job as a business consultant working two days per week, making about 20 percent of her previous income. They sold their huge house and purchased a simple home in a middle-class neighborhood. They also sold their cabin, boat, and two of their four cars. Although their new life proved dramatically different, for Steve and Lisa, less equaled more. They now had time for each other, for Nathan, and for their friends. They also became involved in their community and went back to church. Although they earned substantially less income, life was far richer.

A Perfect Life

Six years later, when Nathan turned seven years old, his second-grade teacher gave her class a unique assignment. She told each student to write a brief essay and to draw a picture depicting their version of a perfect life. Nathan completed the assignment and turned it in to his teacher. After she graded the assignment, Nathan brought it home, along with some math and spelling worksheets. He laid them on the kitchen table and went out to play with his neighborhood friends. Later Lisa sat down at the table and picked up Nathan's papers. As she looked at his "perfect life" assignment, tears began to flow down her face. In fact, she began to weep—not out of sadness but out of joy.

Nathan's perfect life project had three sections. First, he drew a picture of his modest house. The drawing included Nathan, his mom and dad, and his dog. Under the drawing of his house he wrote "My home." To the right of his house he drew a checkerboard with faces inside each square. The caption under the drawing read, "My friends." Next to his friends Nathan drew a picture of a church with a steeple. The caption read, "My church." Under the three pictures of his home, friends, and church, Nathan wrote his brief essay. He said, "A perfect life for me is the life that I'm in right now. I have a lot of friends, and a good family too, and a good church. I do not need a perfect life. I already have a perfect life."

Unlike many Americans, Steve, Lisa, and Nathan have figured out what matters most in life. They've learned that career success, money, big houses, and status cars are not the main thing. Instead, what matters most are our relationships—with God and with others. If we, like Steve and Lisa and Nathan, ever figure that out—not just in our heads but also in our hearts—we'll come much closer to living "a perfect life."

The Bottom Line

In Mark 12 a religious leader asks Jesus, "Of all the commandments, which is the most important?" (v. 28 NIV). In essence, this religious leader asks Jesus, "Of all the things that clamor for our time, energy, and attention, what matters most? What is the bottom line?" It's a crucial question. You and I are constantly bombarded with dozens of concerns, including our job, career, marriage, children, home, friends, faith, church, community, health, and finances. And these concerns often compete with one another for our time and energy. So how do we figure out what matters most? What is primary? What is secondary? What really counts? That's what this religious leader was trying to figure out. He wanted to know—what is the greatest priority of life?

So he asked Jesus, "What matters most?" And Jesus told him. But Jesus didn't mention any of the things that American culture deems important. He didn't talk about career advancement, financial security, physical appearance, health, fame, power, or social status. Instead, Jesus said our life should be focused on relationships—with God and with others. Let's look at the passage.

> One of the scribes came near and heard them disputing with one another, and seeing that he [Jesus] answered them well, he asked him, "Which commandment is the first of all?" Jesus answered, "The first is, 'Hear O Israel: the Lord our God, the Lord is one; and you shall love the Lord your God with all your heart, and with all your soul, and with all your mind, and with all your strength.' The second is this, 'You shall love your neighbor as yourself.' There is no other commandment greater than these." (Mark 12:28–31)

According to Jesus, the greatest priority of life is to love God and neighbor. We call this "the Great Commandment." Relationships—with God and others—is Jesus' bottom line. Jesus taught, lived, and died this priority, and he challenges us to do the same.

I know this is not new to you. It's actually quite elementary. It's theology 101, the ABCs of Christianity. But don't be fooled by its simplicity. Jesus' greatest priority in life is radically different from what our culture teaches us. All the things we worry so much about—houses, stock portfolios, physical health, beauty, social status, and career success—are minor issues according to Jesus. For Jesus, the bottom line is love of God and neighbor. Although I memorized the Great Commandment at age sixteen, it took over twenty years and two epiphanies—one during a late-night movie and another at an Episcopal church—for it finally to sink in. Perhaps my story will help you think about what matters most in your life.

Meeting God at the Movies

During my senior year of college, I went into the insurance business part-time. After graduating, I went full-time. For some reason it clicked. I won numerous sales awards and started making a lot of money. Before long, making money became my greatest priority. So in order to earn even more income, I worked day and night, seven days a week. And it worked. I made an enormous amount of money. But in the process I neglected my family, my health, and my soul. Late one night I came home from another long day of work. My wife and young son were both asleep. I rarely saw them in those days: I was too busy making money. Too wired up to sleep, I turned on the TV and watched the late-night classic movie. That night's selection was *Cat on a Hot Tin Roof*, starring Paul Newman, Burl Ives, and Elizabeth Taylor, based on the Pulitzer Prize-winning play by Tennessee Williams.

Cat on a Hot Tin Roof tells the story of an old man and his family. The man was rich and powerful; everyone called him "Big Daddy." He had all the things money could buy: a big Southern mansion, twenty-eight thousand acres of fertile farmland, and millions of dollars in stocks and bonds. Big Daddy had it all. He also had an alcoholic son, colon cancer, and the certainty of death in the near future. The end of the movie finds Big Daddy and his son in the basement of his mansion. For one brief moment Big Daddy's masks of power, wealth, and success are stripped away. We realize that he's not wealthy at all. He has a shallow relationship with his wife. He is estranged from his son. And his daughter's only concern is getting the lion's share of Big Daddy's estate. He has no significant relationships; he doesn't even know the names of his servants. He knows no love, no purpose in life, no faith, no meaning. He is absolutely bankrupt. What does Big Daddy have? A basement full of expensive European antiques.

Cat on a Hot Tin Roof served as a powerful epiphany for me. I realized that if I continued on my present course, I would end up just like Big Daddy, rich in material things but bankrupt in things that really matter. God used that movie and several other experiences to say, "You are chasing after the wrong dream. Money is not what matters most."

From Chasing Money to Chasing Success

Soon after that experience I left the insurance business, went to seminary, and entered ministry. Making a lot of money was no longer my priority. For a while love of God

and neighbor mattered most. But before long my real passion became my career. Back then, if someone had asked me
what mattered most and I had answered honestly, I would
have said, "Career advancement." As fast as I could, I got
in a bigger church and then an even bigger one. I began to
publish articles and books, earned a doctor's degree, and
jumped on the ministerial speaker's circuit. Then I landed
a status job as a national preaching and worship editor and
consultant for my old denomination. After that, I accepted
a pastorate in a large church in Honolulu.

For fifteen years I became totally consumed with career
success—and managed to attain a measure of it. But it
didn't last long. During my years of ecclesiastical career
climbing, my old denomination shifted from a conservative
yet open-minded stance to being closed-minded and fundamentalist. I'm deeply grateful for my old denomination.
They loved me, introduced me to Jesus, educated me, and
gave me incredible opportunities of service. But tragically,
extremist religious-right, fundamentalist leaders took control. And while I can be many things, I cannot be a fundamentalist Christian. So in the summer of 1994, at the top of
my career, I resigned my church in Hawaii, sold my surf-
boards, and left my old denomination. Devastated over the
collapse of my career and uncertain about what to do next,
my family and I moved to Nashville, where I began PhD
studies in worship and preaching at Vanderbilt University.

Ambushed by God at Christ Episcopal Church

Then in October of 1994, I had an experience that changed
my life forever. In my search for a new denomination, I visited a worship service at Christ Episcopal Church in Nashville. The Episcopalians made my short list of possible

new church homes, along with the Presbyterians and the United Methodists. So I went to Christ Church that October morning to check out the Episcopal Church. At the time I felt tremendous grief and depression over the loss of my career and was confused about what to do next. I walked into the sanctuary of Christ Church that morning wounded and broken. And on that day I encountered the living God.

The Scripture reading that morning came from Mark 12, the Great Commandment of Jesus. I don't remember the details, but the sermon, preached by a woman minister, affirmed Jesus' priority of loving God and neighbor. The service and sermon served as a wake-up call from God. Through that worship service God said to me, "Martin, your career is not what matters most. Indeed, your obsession with career advancement has become idolatry. What matters most is not your career but relationships — with me and with others." As I prayed, cried, sang, and took Holy Communion, I came to see the one thing that mattered most. And it wasn't career advancement. What mattered most was loving God and loving others.

I've not been the same since that Sunday in October 1994. Since then, loving God and neighbor has become far more important to me than career success. And life is far sweeter as a result. My career ambition is no longer to get a bigger church or a status denominational job. My only career goal is to be a Great Commandment pastor. More than anything else, I want to love God and others, especially the people in my congregation and community. And my personal goal as a husband, father, and friend is to be a Great Commandment person. Above everything else, I want to love God, and I want to love the people in my life. Why? Because according to Jesus Christ our Lord, that's what matters most; that is the bottom line.

What about My Résumé?

Years ago I met an exceptionally gifted and extremely ambitious young minister named Ron. If you had asked Ron what mattered most, and he had been honest, he would have said, "Building up an impressive résumé." And he did. Ron has all kinds of degrees, including a PhD. He wrote and published numerous articles and even a book. He serves as an adjunct professor of theology at a seminary. He pastors a large, status church. He's on all kinds of important boards and committees and has been awarded many honors in his community. Ron's résumé is about five pages long, listing accomplishment after accomplishment.

Several years ago, when I was teaching a seminary class in Ron's town, he and I had a conversation. A few weeks earlier Ron had undergone serious back surgery, from which he was still recovering. During our visit Ron told me about his back surgery. After the surgery Ron dreamed a strange dream. In his dream he died and met God. And when he did, God surprised him. Ron said, "In my dream God didn't ask me one thing about my résumé. God didn't ask me about my degrees, my publications, my speaking engagements, or my denominational work. God didn't even ask me how large my church was. I mean — God didn't say one word about my résumé! Instead, God asked only one question: "Ron, did you love me with all your heart, soul, mind, and strength, and did you love your neighbor as yourself?"

❈ ❈ ❈

Bottom line: *Relationships — with God and others — matter most.*

CHAPTER 13

⬱⬱

JESUS' GRACE

Am I Accepted?

*Jesus . . . said to her, "Woman, where are they? Has no one con-
demned you? She said, "No one, sir." And Jesus said, "Neither do I
condemn you."*

—John 8:10–11

Several decades ago, a group of theologians gathered
in England for a conference on comparative religions.
They grappled with the question "Is there one belief completely unique to the Christian faith?"

As they debated that question, world-famous theologian and author C. S. Lewis walked into the room. "What's
going on?" he asked.

Someone told him that his colleagues were discussing
the question "Is there one belief unique to Christianity?"

C. S. Lewis responded, "Oh, that's easy: it's grace."

By the end of the conference, the theologians agreed with
Lewis. God's unconditional grace, offered to human beings
with no strings attached, is indeed unique in the world's

religions. Buddhists follow an eightfold path to righteousness. Hindus believe in the doctrine of karma. Jews, in order to receive God's blessings, must obey God's covenant. Islam has a strict code of law that all Muslims must follow. In one way or another, every religion of the world requires people to earn God's approval—every religion except Christianity. The one belief that is completely unique to the Christian faith is grace: God's unconditional love and acceptance of us just as we are.[1] Of course, some Christian groups have added additional requirements to the baseline of God's unconditional grace. But at its core, pure Christianity is all about the "Amazing Grace" of God. That grace, more than anything else, draws people to Christianity.

God's Job Description

That proved true for Anne Lamott. In her irreverent yet delightful book *Traveling Mercies*, Anne shares her journey toward faith in Jesus Christ. Anne's story of faith is mostly a story about being drawn to God's grace. Years ago Anne found herself broke, drunk, bulimic, depressed, and addicted to drugs. She said, "I could no longer imagine how God could love me." Desperate, Anne set an appointment with an Episcopal priest.

She told him, "I'm so messed up that I don't think God can love me."

The priest replied, "God *has* to love you. That's God's job."[2]

Anne's priest was absolutely right. God works full-time offering unconditional love to all human beings. God's affirming and forgiving love, what theologians call "grace," is God's best gift to humanity. Grace means that in spite of all our flaws, failures, and sins, God dearly loves us and offers us forgiveness. As renegade Baptist preacher Will

Campbell once put it, "We're all bastards, but God loves us anyway." Although crude, that statement rings true. Every human being fails to live up to God's standards. However, in spite of that, God continues to offer us grace upon grace.

Party for a Prostitute

My favorite story about God's grace comes from Tony Campolo, a well-known author and speaker. I heard him tell it at a conference in Honolulu. You may have heard this story before: it's becoming quite famous. However, even if you're familiar with Tony's story, it's worth retelling.

Years ago, Tony traveled to Honolulu to speak at a conference. Upon arriving, Tony went to his hotel and fell asleep. He woke at 9:00 a.m. his time, but in Honolulu it was 3:00 a.m. Wide awake and hungry, Tony walked to a small diner near the hotel and ordered coffee and a doughnut. At 3:30 a.m., a group of provocatively dressed prostitutes walked in the door. Their loud and crude talk made Tony uncomfortable, so he prepared to leave.

But then he heard one of the women say, "Tomorrow's my birthday. I'm going to be thirty-nine."

Her friend responded, "So what do you want from me, a birthday party? You want me to get you a cake and sing 'Happy Birthday'?"

"Come on!" said the woman. "Why do you have to be so mean? I was just telling you, that's all. I don't want anything from you. I mean, why should you give me a birthday party? I've never had a birthday party in my whole life. Why should I have one now?"

When Tony heard those words, he made a decision. He stayed in the diner until the women left. Then he said to the owner, "Do they come in here every night?"

"Yeah," he said. "You can set your clock by it."

Tony said, "What's the name of the woman who sat next to me?"

"That's Agnes," he replied.

Tony said, "What do you think about us throwing a birthday party for her — right here — tomorrow night?"

A smile crossed the owner's face, and he said, "That's great! I like it! I'll even make the cake."

At 2:00 the next morning, Tony went back to the diner. He put up crepe-paper decorations and a big sign: HAPPY BIRTHDAY, AGNES! The workers at the diner obviously got the word out because by 3:15 just about every prostitute in Honolulu crowded into the place. At 3:30 sharp, the door swung open, and in came Agnes and her friends.

Tony had the entire group scream, "Happy birthday, Agnes!" Agnes, absolutely stunned, felt so overwhelmed her friend had to hold her up. Everyone in the diner began to sing, "Happy Birthday to You."

When they brought out the cake covered with thirty-nine candles, Agnes began to cry. Too overcome with emotion to blow out the candles, she let the owner of the diner blow them out for her. Before she cut the cake, Agnes hesitated. She asked if she could take her cake down the street, show it to her mother, and then come right back. The owner of the diner said that would be fine, so she did.

When the door closed behind Agnes, silence filled the diner. Tony broke the silence by saying, "What do you say we pray?" It probably seemed strange for a roomful of prostitutes to bow their heads in prayer, but that's what happened. Tony prayed for Agnes and for the other prostitutes in the diner, affirming that they were beloved daughters of God, with great value, worth, and promise.

When Tony finished the prayer, the owner of the diner said, "You never told me you were a preacher. What kind of church do you belong to?"

In a moment of divine inspiration, Tony said, "I belong to a church that throws birthday parties for prostitutes at 3:30 in the morning."[3]

Friend of Sinners

I love Tony's story because it reminds me so much of Jesus. Rather than judge people, Jesus loved and accepted them. We see a vivid example of this in John 8. In this story a woman is caught in the act of adultery. Religious authorities bring her (but not the man) to Jesus, demanding that she be stoned to death, in accord with Jewish law (vv. 3–6).

Jesus says to them, "Let anyone among you who is without sin be the first to throw a stone at her" (v. 7).

One by one they slip away from the scene, leaving their stones behind (v. 9).

Jesus asks, "Woman, where are they? Has no one condemned you?" (v. 10).

She replies, "No one, sir."

And Jesus says, "Neither do I condemn you" (v. 11).

The Bible contains numerous stories about Jesus' spending time with and offering grace to flawed people, including adulterers, prostitutes, tax collectors, and other sinners. The Pharisees, a group of self-righteous and judgmental religious leaders, vigorously complain about that, as we see in this passage from the Gospel of Matthew:

> And as he [Jesus] sat at dinner in the house, many tax collectors and sinners came and were sitting with him and his disciples. When the Pharisees saw this, they said to his disciples, "Why does your teacher eat with tax collectors and sinners?" But when he heard this, he said, "Those who are well have no need of a physician, but those who

are sick. Go and learn what this means, 'I desire mercy, not sacrifice.' For I have come to call not the righteous but sinners." (9:10–13)

At his core, Jesus was a man of mercy and grace. He consistently loved, accepted, and welcomed imperfect sinful people into God's family. It's not that Jesus approved of sinful behavior: not at all. For example, when Jesus offered forgiveness and grace to the woman caught in adultery mentioned above, he told her, "Go now and leave your life of sin" (John 8:11 NIV). Jesus did not condone sinfulness. He did not lay aside the Ten Commandments. Yet Jesus loved sinners, accepted them, and welcomed them as they were. In spite of their sin, Jesus refused to judge and condemn them. Instead, Jesus saw them as beloved children of God, created in the image of God, with great value and worth. Obviously Jesus hoped they would change for the better. He wanted them to grow in morality and purity. But even with their flaws, Jesus warmly welcomed sinners and offered them forgiveness, love, and acceptance. In short, Jesus offered them grace. He does the same for you and me.

Not only did Jesus live out God's grace; he also told wonderful stories about God's grace. Perhaps the most famous example is Jesus' parable of the Prodigal Son found in Luke 15. In that story an arrogant son demands his inheritance from his father. He then takes the money, leaves home, and squanders his inheritance on sinful living. After going broke, the boy returns home, tail between his legs. In spite of everything, the father welcomes the boy back home with love, forgiveness, and even celebration. In this parable Jesus teaches us that God is like a loving parent who grants amnesty to his or her sinful children. In short, Jesus teaches us that God is a God of grace.

Jesus lived out grace. Jesus taught grace. Even Jesus' death was grace filled. When the authorities and crowd condemned, mocked, and crucified him, Jesus offered them grace, saying, "Father, forgive them; for they do not know what they are doing" (Luke 23:34). On the cross, even though he was suffering in agony, Jesus took time to hear the confession of the dying thief hanging next to him. Jesus offered him grace, saying, "Today you will be with me in Paradise" (Luke 23:43). Grace—more than any other trait—defined Jesus' life, his teachings, and even his death.

Jesus' Theme Song

If Jesus had a theme song, it would be "Amazing Grace." As you may know, this famous hymn was written back in 1779 by a former slave trader named John Newton. In spite of his horrendous sins in the slave trade, Newton experienced the forgiving and transforming grace of God. Thus he could say, "Amazing grace! How sweet the sound / that saved a wretch like me! / I once was lost, but now am found, / was blind, but now I see." Because of Jesus' amazing grace, sinners like the woman caught in adultery, the prodigal son, John Newton, and you and me can know God's love, forgiveness, and acceptance. As the Gospel of John says, "For God so loved the world that he gave his only Son, so that everyone who believes in him may not perish but may have eternal life. Indeed, God did not send the Son into the world to condemn the world, but in order that the world might be saved through him" (3:16–17).

However, this does *not* mean that we can accept God's grace and then live any way we please. That would be, in Dietrich Bonhoeffer's words, "cheap grace." Yes, God loves us as we are. However, God wants us to become *more* than we are. Once we accept God's grace, God expects us to live differently. As beloved children of God, we are called to live like God's children—full of integrity, love, morality, and spiritual maturity. As we say in the United Methodist Church, we must move from "justifying grace" (grace that makes us right with God) to "sanctifying grace" (grace that leads to spiritual maturity). In the words of John Wesley, founder of the Methodist movement, after we receive God's grace, we must "move on toward perfection." For a more-thorough discussion of this important subject, see chapter 21, "A Final Question: Do Mainline Christians Believe in Getting Saved?"

Dancing with Grace

Several months ago I watched an old movie called *Awakenings*, starring Robin Williams and Robert De Niro. Produced back in 1990, it won Academy Awards for Best Picture, Best Actor, and Best Adapted Screenplay. It's a true and touching story about a group of catatonic patients at a mental hospital who had lived in a coma-like existence for decades. However, through the use of a new drug, a caring doctor woke the patients out of their catatonic existence. Among them was a man named Leonard. After decades of living in a vegetative state, Leonard awakened to life. As the movie unfolds, we delight in Leonard's progress and learn that he is an intelligent, sensitive, and loving human being.

As the weeks progressed, Leonard made friends with a woman who regularly came to the hospital to visit her father. She and Leonard hit it off and became fast friends. However, as the story unfolds, Leonard began to regress.

The miracle medicine slowly lost its effectiveness. Leonard began to develop tics all over his face and body, and he knows it's only a matter of time before he returns to his catatonic state. Before long the tics become so overwhelming that it's difficult to watch him anymore. Still, the woman continued her friendship with Leonard. She accepted him as he was, even with his awful twitches. She still valued him as a human being, cared about him, and affirmed him. In short, she gave Leonard the wonderful gift of grace.

Near the end of the movie, Leonard had lunch with this woman. As they ate, she told Leonard about a dance she had recently attended. Leonard replied that he had never danced before and probably never would. After lunch they both stood. As Leonard prepared to leave, he reached out his trembling arm to shake hands with her, probably for the last time. She took his hand but would not let go. Instead, she put Leonard's arms around her in a dance position and held him closely. And there, on the cafeteria floor of the state mental hospital, she and Leonard began to dance. As they danced, the camera focused on Leonard's face—beaming with joy in an incredible moment of grace.

As I watched this remarkable woman dance with Leonard, I thought to myself, *This is the way it is with God and human beings*. Like Leonard, every human being twitches with flaws and sins and brokenness. And yet God, like this woman, holds us close with compassionate unconditional love and dances with us across the floor. I don't remember the woman's name. But I'd like to think her name was Grace.

❖ ❖ ❖

Bottom line: *Even with our flaws, Jesus loves and accepts us as beloved children of God.*

Notes for Chapter 13

1. Philip Yancey, *What's So Amazing about Grace?* (Grand Rapids: Zondervan, 1997), 45.

2. Anne Lamott, *Traveling Mercies: Some Thoughts on Faith* (New York: Anchor Books, 1999), 43.

3. Tony Campolo, *Let Me Tell You a Story: Life Lessons from Unexpected Places and Unlikely People* (Nashville: Thomas Nelson, 2000), 216–20.

CHAPTER 14

∞∽∞

JESUS' WORK

Where Is God?

And the Word became flesh and lived among us.

—John 1:14

Every August at my church is Faith and Film month. We take a diverse selection of movies, both religious and secular, and use them to illustrate biblical truths. Last year one of our Faith and Film messages was "God at Work: Two Views." On that Sunday we used two films to help answer the question "How does God work in the world?"

The first film was *The Truman Show* starring Jim Carrey. This unique movie tells the story of a reality TV show that stars a young man named Truman Burbank. Although Truman doesn't know it, every detail of his life is being broadcast to millions of people around the globe twenty-four hours a day, seven days a week. From birth, Truman's every move has been captured on film by thousands of hidden cameras. Truman lives in a massive television studio enclosed in a huge dome, which replicates a small island town called Seahaven. The director of the show, a man named Christof, controls everything in Truman's life. He picks Truman's friends, his job, his girlfriends, and even his wife—all of whom, unknown to Truman, are actors on *The Truman Show*. Christof even controls the weather. He makes day and night, rain and wind, sunshine and stars. After showing a brief clip from the film, I told our congregation that a lot of people think God works in the world like Christof does on *The Truman Show*. They believe that God directly controls all the details of life on earth, including weather patterns and human decisions.

For a second view of how God works in the world, we turned to a movie called *Apollo 13*. This Academy Award-winning film starring Tom Hanks tells the true story of NASA's troubled flight to the moon in April 1970. Almost everything that can go wrong on that mission does go wrong. Prospects look bleak for the crew. As the days progress, it appears likely that the astronauts of *Apollo 13* will perish in space. In response to that grave situation, millions of people around the globe fervently pray to God for their safe return. The pope even says a special mass on their behalf. In the end God answers their prayers. Against all odds, the crew of *Apollo 13* survives. However, God does not save the crew in a direct, supernatural way. Instead, God saves them through human instruments. God uses the wisdom, skills, and persistence of dedicated NASA engineers and scientists to get them safely home again.

After showing a clip from *Apollo 13*, I asked my congregation, "Does God work in the world like Christof in *The Truman Show*, directly controlling the details of human existence? Or does God work in the world indirectly, through human instruments, as suggested in *Apollo 13*?"

In the end, as I acknowledged to my congregation, it's not an either/or question. God is God and can do whatever

God wants. If God wants to directly control events in the world, God can certainly choose to do so. However, the Bible teaches us that God *primarily* works in the world through human instruments. In short, God's involvement in the world resembles *Apollo 13* far more than it resembles *The Truman Show*. To illustrate that point, let me share a real-life example.

God of Blankets and Baby Formula

Several years ago tornadoes ravaged the town of Lafayette in my home state of Tennessee, destroying both property and lives. Two days after the tornadoes hit, a person from our congregation dropped by my office. He wanted to talk about the awful tragedy in Lafayette. During our conversation he asked, "Pastor, when terrible things like this happen, where is God?"

I said, "Come with me, and I'll show you where God is." Then I took him to our Family Life Center, where people busily loaded supplies into a large truck. The day before, we sent out a congregation-wide telephone message, asking our members to donate needed supplies for the community of Lafayette. People came out of the woodwork, bringing nonperishable food, blankets, clothes, diapers, baby formula, and bottled water. In fact, they brought an entire truckload of supplies. They also brought lots of money, and a good number of them volunteered their time and energy to personally help with relief efforts.

I said to my church member, "You asked me, 'Where is God?' Well, God is right here, in the midst of all this food, clothing, diapers, baby formula, and bottled water."

The next day a group of men from a Nashville church showed up in tornado-ravaged Lafayette with chainsaws and pickup trucks. They spent the next three days cutting

up fallen trees and hauling the debris away. A newspaper
reporter interviewed one of the men with the chainsaws.
Although this blue-collar construction worker did not
have a seminary degree, I'd give him an A+ in theology.
When the reporter asked him why he and his friends came
to help, he said, "We want to be God with skin on."

I don't pretend to have all the answers to the question
"Where is God?" God is bigger and more mysterious than
any of us can comprehend. No doubt God works in the
world in ways our puny minds cannot even begin to understand. The life and work of Jesus, however, clearly teaches
us that God primarily works *through people*.

"The Word Became Flesh"

We see this truth throughout the Bible. Scripture makes
abundantly clear that God is present and active in the world
through human beings. God worked through Adam and
Eve to name the animals and tend the garden. God worked
through Sarah and Abraham to give birth to the Jewish
nation. God worked through Moses to set the people of
Israel free from oppressive slavery. God worked through
King David to establish the nation of Israel. God challenged the Israelites to "let justice roll down like waters"
through Amos (5:24) and other Old Testament prophets.

And when God wanted to do God's most important
work ever, God did so through a young woman named
Mary, who gave birth to Jesus Christ. In perhaps the most
important passage of the New Testament, the Bible says,
"And the Word became flesh and lived among us" (John
1:14). The theological term for that is *incarnation*: it means
"God became flesh."

In short, the incarnation tells us that God actively
engages in the world through human beings, especially

through Jesus Christ. When Jesus first embarked upon his public ministry, he went to his home synagogue in Nazareth and read these words from the book of Isaiah, which laid out his lifework:

> The Spirit of the Lord is upon me,
>   because he has anointed me
>   to bring good news to the poor.
> He has sent me to proclaim release to the captives
>   and recovery of sight to the blind,
>   to let the oppressed go free,
> to proclaim the year of the Lord's favor.
>
> *(Luke 4:18–19)*

Jesus spent the next three years living out that text. However, he didn't do his work alone: he recruited others to help. His first order of business was to gather a group of disciples to help him carry out his mission. Those disciples recruited more people to help carry out Christ's work, then those folks recruited even more people. That same pattern has continued for over two thousand years. As modern-day disciples, we are part of that tradition. As the "body of Christ," we are called to be Jesus' hands, arms, feet, and heart. Our task as Christ's church is to carry on the mission of our Lord. When we do, we are a part of God's continuing incarnational work in the world.

I saw this reality lived out a few weeks ago when I attended the dedication ceremony for our congregation's most recent Habitat for Humanity build. Seventy people showed up, all of whom had played a role in building and/ or financing the house. During the ceremony the woman receiving the home gave a brief thank-you speech. She said to the crowd, "God provided this home for my family and me. But God used all of you to make it happen." Although she's not a trained theologian, she understands well the theology of incarnation: God works in the world through human instruments.

God at Work

As the pastor of a local congregation, I get to see God work through people all the time. For example, when members of our congregation take Communion to elderly shut-ins every month or feed and tutor at-risk children in the local housing project, God is at work. When people in our community schedule appointments with our church counselor and find hope for their marriage or healing for their addiction, God is at work. When teachers in our congregation educate children at school or when our doctors and nurses help people get well, God is at work. When businesspeople in our church create jobs in the community, allowing workers to provide for their families, God is at work. When parents in our church safely tuck their children in at night with a loving kiss and a prayer, God is at work.

When our members donate food to our community food pantry, volunteer at our local homeless shelter, or give blood at our Red Cross blood drives, God is at work. When a group of women in our church gather every Wednesday morning to knit sweaters for children in poverty, or when our lay Stephen Ministers reach out to hurting people in our community, God is at work. When large numbers of our congregation sponsor impoverished children through Compassion International or help fight poverty through Heifer International, God is at work. When a group of our folks go to Mexico every Christmas to minister with the poorest of the poor, God is at work. When our members invite unchurched people to our church and those people come to faith in Jesus Christ and connect with our church family, God is at work. When our congregation raises large amounts of money for disaster relief after such events as 9/11, the Indonesian Tsunami (2004), Hurricane Katrina (2005), and the Haiti earthquake (2010), God is at work.

And that's just one church in one little town. That same dynamic is happening in powerful ways throughout the entire world. When people fight for justice on behalf of the oppressed and serve as advocates of the poor, God is at work. When the hungry are fed, the naked clothed, the sick cared for, and the illiterate educated, God is at work. When leaders seek peace instead of war, when people fight to protect the environment, and when scientists discover new drugs to fight debilitating diseases, God is at work. When the gospel is shared all over the world and new churches are born, God is at work. When people from all over the world respond to the devastating earthquake crisis in Haiti with love, compassion, and practical aid, surely God is at work.

Who Will Be Jesus?

Years ago Bruce Carroll wrote a song called "Who Will Be Jesus?" In the song, Bruce tells stories about struggling people who desperately need the love, support, and encouragement of God. He concludes, "They do not need a judge: they need a friend. Who will be Jesus to them?" When we are Jesus to people in need, when we offer them grace, love, compassion, support, and practical help, we are instruments of God's incarnational work in the world.

So where is God? Jesus' life and work teaches us that God is at work in the world *incarnationally* — through *human instruments*, including you and me. Imagine that!

I once heard a story about a woman who locked her keys in her car in a rough part of town. She found an old coat hanger lying on the street and tried to break in, but with no success. Feeling desperate, she finally prayed, "Dear God, please send somebody to help me." Within five minutes an old rusty car pulled up. A rough-looking, tattooed, bearded man wearing a biker skull rag walked toward her. She thought, *Great Scott! This is who God sent to help me?* But she was desperate. So when the man asked if he could help, she said, "Can you help me break into my car?"

He said, "Sure, I'm good at that." He took the coat hanger, walked over to her car, and in thirty seconds flat opened the door.

She hugged the man and said, "Thank you so much. You are a very nice man."

He replied, "Lady, I'm not a nice man. I got out of prison just today. I served two years for auto theft and have only been out for about an hour."

The woman hugged the man again and shouted, with great enthusiasm, "Thank you, God, for sending me a professional!"

※　※　※

Bottom line: *Although God is not limited to working through people, God primarily works through human instruments.*

CHAPTER 15

◌◌◌

JESUS' EXAMPLE

What Brings Fulfillment?

> *Then he [Jesus] poured water into a basin and began to wash the disciples' feet and to wipe them with the towel that was tied around him.*
>
> —John 13:5

Even as a boy, Millard Fuller excelled at business and finance. When Millard turned thirteen, his father, a farmer, gave him a pet pig. Millard, already an entrepreneur, bred his pet pig with other pigs on the farm and became a teenage livestock trader. During high school he made enough money selling livestock to pay his entire four years of college. While attending law school, Millard went into partnership with a friend, marketing various products. They plowed most of their profits into real estate. During his final year of law school Millard made $50,000 from his various business interests. Upon graduation, he set up a successful law practice. On the side Millard went into the cookbook and mail-order business with phenomenal success.

During law school Millard fell in love with and married a woman named Linda. Within a few years Millard and Linda had two beautiful children. They later added two more. Millard was now in his early thirties. His success in business made him a millionaire. He owned a luxurious home, a vacation retreat, boats, cars, and significant assets in three cattle ranches. Already successful and rich, Millard now had a picture-perfect family. He seemingly had everything a person could wish for—youth, success, money, health, marriage, children, and status in the community. At a young age he achieved the American dream. If anybody should be happy, content, and fulfilled, it would be Millard Fuller.

Disillusioned with the American Dream

But Millard and Linda were not fulfilled. One day Linda dropped by Millard's office and told him she didn't think she loved him anymore. Millard's brush with divorce resulted in some serious soul-searching in his life. Over the next few months, Millard and Linda made several important decisions. First, they decided not to get a divorce. Instead, they vowed to stick together and work out their problems. Second, they realized that their possessions had not enriched them but enslaved them. So they made the radical decision to give away their belongings and start fresh. They sold their business and most of their assets, then gave the proceeds—over a million dollars—to charity. Finally, they decided to devote their lives to serving other people. For years they had served only themselves; now they wanted to serve others. It's a long story, but Millard and Linda eventually founded an organization called Habitat for Humanity. As you probably know, Habitat for Humanity is a Christian organization that helps working poor people get decent housing.

Years ago, before his retirement and eventual death, I heard Millard speak at a Habitat for Humanity rally in Cookeville, Tennessee. He told the crowd that he experienced far more fulfillment working for Habitat than he ever did making millions of dollars in business. Millard said, "The happiest, most satisfied, and most fulfilled people I know are concerned about something bigger than themselves." When Millard and Linda Fuller moved beyond their own selfish interests and began serving others, they discovered joy and contentment in their lives. We're no different. If we want to be truly fulfilled, we must find ways to serve.

He Took a Towel

That brings me back to Jesus. Let's look at one of the most important stories ever told about our Lord.

> So he got up from the meal, took off his outer clothing, and wrapped a towel around his waist. After that, he poured water into a basin and began to wash his disciples' feet, drying them with the towel that was wrapped around him. . . . When he had finished washing their feet, he put on his clothes and returned to his place. "Do you understand what I have done for you?" he asked them. "You call me 'Teacher' and 'Lord,' and rightly so, for that is what I am. Now that I, your Lord and Teacher, have washed your feet, you should wash one another's feet. I have set you an example that you should do as I have done for you. . . . Now that you know these things, you will be blessed if you do them. (John 13:4–5, 12–15, 17 NIV)

In this passage and throughout the entire New Testament, Jesus teaches us that service to others is a key ingredient of a rewarding life. By taking on the role of a servant and washing his disciple's feet, Jesus shows us that true fulfillment comes from caring for others. As Jesus said in this text, when we follow his example and serve other people, we "will be blessed" (v. 17 NIV). Jesus dedicated his entire life to service. He lived and died in the service of humanity. When we, like Jesus, take up our towel and wash other people's feet, that's when we'll find real life.

I cannot overemphasize how important this is. Self-absorbed people who live only for themselves and their immediate family will never be content. Self is too small a god to serve. True fulfillment comes only through service to others. Hundreds of different ways exist for us to follow Jesus' example. But every Christian is called by God to pick up a towel and wash the feet of others in some way. And when we do, we—like Millard Fuller of Habitat for Humanity—will discover true joy and fulfillment.

From the Oval Office to Scrubbing Toilets

It's difficult to think of Millard Fuller without also thinking of President Jimmy Carter. Carter, more than anyone else, helped make Habitat for Humanity famous. After leaving the White House, Jimmy Carter devoted his life to serving others. He and his wife, Rosalynn, established the Carter Center in Atlanta, which engages in remarkable service projects all over the world. For example, the Carter Center targeted a handful of diseases that chronically plague poor nations, then mobilized human and financial resources to tackle them. As a result, both guinea worms and river blindness have been nearly eliminated. Carter occasionally serves as a mediator for groups and countries experiencing conflict. He and Rosalynn also support worldwide childhood immunization programs. But it's not just elaborate service projects that Jimmy Carter engages in. He also performs ordinary, mundane service. For example, Carter spends a lot of his time at Habitat for Humanity construction sites, hammering nails and carrying lumber. He teaches Sunday school at his church every Sunday. And every other month he and Rosalynn take their turn mowing the grass and cleaning the bathrooms at their little church in Plains, Georgia.

Jimmy Carter was once the most powerful person on the planet. He entertained presidents and kings at the White House. He controlled nuclear weapons that could destroy the planet. Today Jimmy Carter fights childhood diseases, negotiates peace, hammers nails for Habitat houses, teaches Sunday school classes, and mows grass and scrubs toilets at his church.

When Jimmy Carter left the White House, he could have retired in leisure or made lots of money on the speaking circuit. Instead, he and his wife devoted themselves to service. That service pleases God. It also deeply enriches their life. Barbara Walters once interviewed Jimmy Carter on TV. She asked him to think back on his remarkable life as an engineer, naval officer, peanut farmer, governor, and finally president of the United States of America. She asked him, "What phase of your life did you most enjoy?" He thought about it for a moment, smiled a big smile, and said, "Now."

Dr. Green's Final Prescription

Like millions of other Americans, I was a fan of the long-running television show *ER*. This engaging medical drama told the story of the staff and patients at the emergency room of a fictitious hospital in Chicago. The series ran for fifteen years, from 1994 to 2009, an eternity for a TV show. My favorite *ER* character was Dr. Mark Green, played by Anthony Edwards. In the show Dr. Green developed a brain tumor. In spite of the best medical treatments available, the tumor proved to be inoperable. Dr. Green had only a few weeks left to live. So Mark, along with his wife and daughter, went to Hawaii, where he had lived as a kid while his dad served in the Navy. Mark always loved Hawaii and decided that's where he wanted to die. Before his death Dr. Green spoke his last words to his daughter, giving her his final fatherly advice. He thought long and hard about what to tell her and finally came up with the words he wanted to share. The day before he died, Dr. Green gave his final advice, his final prescription, so to speak, to his daughter. He said to her, "Be generous. Be generous with your time. Be generous with your love. Be generous with your life. Be generous."

I'm not sure what final advice I would give my two children if I knew I was about to die. But it would be hard to improve on Dr. Green's final words. Although he was not a particularly religious man, Dr. Green's "final prescription" was deeply spiritual. Throughout the Bible, God encourages all of us to be generous. God wants us to be generous with our time, our love, our compassion, our money, and our service. And when we are generous, when we give of ourselves in service to others, we will find true contentment and fulfillment. As Jesus told his disciples after washing their feet, if you serve others as I have served you, "you will be blessed" (John 13:17 NIV). Proverbs 11:25 puts it this way, "A generous person will be enriched, and one who gives water will get water." The key to a fulfilling life is service to others. And as we see in the following story, it's never too late to begin.

"Who's Taking Care of That Kid?"

Gus learned about the joy of service late in his life. Dying with inoperable cancer, Gus went to a hospice facility. Upon arrival, Gus felt fearful and angry. "Why did I get cancer?" he asked, as if for some strange reason he should be exempt from the disease. "What does God have against me?"

One day Gus stomped down the corridor of the hospice unit, angry that he had not received the service he demanded. An event then happened that transformed his remaining months of life. As he walked down the hall, Gus saw a five-year-old kid. He couldn't believe his eyes: a five-year-old in hospice care.

He went to a nurse and said, "What is that kid doing here? This is a place where old people die, not little kids."

The nurse explained: "The child fell off a tractor, temporarily cutting off oxygen to her brain. The accident resulted in paralysis. She cannot talk or see. However, she is able to hear and respond to simple instructions."

Gus stared at her through the doorway. He couldn't fathom how something like this could happen. "She's only five years old," he said repeatedly. He later learned that her parents lived six hundred miles away and could visit only on weekends.

The next morning Gus again walked by the child's room. "Who's taking care of that kid?" he shouted at the nurses.

After his outburst a nurse replied, "Maybe you ought to do it."

Shocked at the thought, he went back to his room. But he couldn't shake the question from his mind: *Who's taking care of that kid?* Later that evening Gus put on his slippers and went into her room. He said hello to her, but she made no response. He tried speaking to her a second time but, again, nothing. Finally he reached out, touched her hand, and took hold of one of her fingers. As he did, the little girl squeezed his hand. And in that moment Gus was transformed from a bitter, fearful, angry person to one who could love and serve a five-year-old child.

For weeks, Gus and the little girl "talked" to each other through handshakes. He read her stories and played her favorite music. He found a little red wagon, propped her safely in it, and took her on trips around the hospital. As time passed, they developed an intricate language of communication as they snapped their fingers back and forth.

"When Gus died," said a nurse, "he died smiling. He was no longer Gus the fearful patient. Now he was Gus the friend of a five-year-old."[1]

❈ ❈ ❈

Bottom line: *True fulfillment comes from serving others*.

Note for Chapter 15

1. Retold from Robert Veninga, *A Gift of Hope: How We Survive Our Tragedies* (New York: Ballantine Books, 1985), 277–78.

CHAPTER 16

⁀⁀⁀

JESUS' DEATH

What about Suffering?

> *My God, my God, why have you forsaken me?*
> —Jesus, in Matthew 27:46

S t. Mary's congregation gathered on Friday evening for their annual Good Friday worship service. After several lay Scripture readings on the passion of Christ, the guest speaker walked to the pulpit. The preacher, a visiting monk, looked at the congregation but said nothing. After a lengthy moment of silence, he picked up a large candle and then walked to a statue depicting Jesus hanging on the cross. The statue, placed in a dark corner of the church, could barely be seen in the evening light. The monk lifted the candle to Christ's head, illuminating the crown of thorns. He then placed the candle near the outstretched arms of Christ, shedding light on one nail-scarred hand and then the other. Next he placed the candle near the side of Christ, exposing the wound from the soldier's spear. Finally he placed the candle at the bottom of the statue so the congregation could see the stake pounded into Christ's feet. With that he blew out the candle and dismissed the service.

At the center of Christianity hangs a crucified God. The New Testament devotes more space to Jesus' passion and death than any other aspect of his life. Clearly Jesus' suffering is central to Christian faith. Although the cross of Jesus is an ugly scene of brokenness, pain, and death, it is also a picture of God: not a God of glory and majesty, but a God of suffering who, in physical and spiritual agony, cried out from the cross, "My God, my God, why have you forsaken me?" (Matthew 27:46). For over two thousand years, in the midst of endless suffering, Jesus' followers, like him, still ask, "Why?"

Hard Questions

A retired pastor once told about the first and last questions he received in pastoral ministry. The first question came during the first week of his first pastorate. A young couple in his church had an automobile accident, severely injuring their young daughter. She died the next day. During his visit with the family after the child's death, the young mother asked, "Why didn't God let my little girl live?"

The last question came forty years later, during the last week of his last pastorate. He went to visit a severely ill woman in the nursing home. When he arrived, her son was there. In the hallway after the visit, the son talked to this pastor about his mother's long illness and suffering. He asked the pastor, "Why doesn't God let my mother die?"

"Why didn't God let my little girl live?" "Why doesn't God let my mother die?" And in between that first and last question were a thousand other *why* questions. Why did my wife leave me? Why did I get cancer? Why didn't I get a promotion? Why won't my depression go away? Why does God allow hurricanes, tornadoes, earthquakes, and tsunamis? We all have our *why* questions.

I don't pretend to have easy answers to suffering. Such answers don't exist. Still, the questions must be asked. Why does God allow suffering? And where is God when suffering occurs?

Why Does God Allow Suffering?

Several years ago I took a survey of my congregation. I asked them to list topics they wanted me to preach on during an upcoming Pew to Pulpit sermon series. By far the most requested topic was some version of the question "Why does God allow so much suffering in the world?"

It's not a new question. The people of God have asked that question from the very beginning. The entire book of Job grapples with the problem of suffering. Unfortunately Job does not answer the question "Why does God allow suffering?" Why not? I think it's because there is no final answer, at least not one that our finite minds can comprehend. As Paul once said, "We know only in part" and "We see through the glass dimly" (see 1 Corinthians 13:9, 12). We don't have all the answers about suffering, and at least in this life, we never will. So as we struggle with the problem of pain, we must admit our ignorance. One day God will make all things clear; but for now we have limited perspective.

However, we do have *some* answers as to why suffering occurs. For example, a huge amount of suffering is caused by human sin. From creation, God gifted human beings with free will. Sadly, we often abuse that freedom and make terrible choices that result in suffering. A man smokes three packs of cigarettes a day and develops lung cancer and emphysema. A young person gets drunk, drives her car on the highway, and kills an entire family. A greedy dictator, in an effort to grab more land, declares war on another nation, killing thousands. A terrorist wraps his body with explosives, walks into a busy marketplace, and kills dozens of innocent people. Sin causes untold suffering, including terrorism, torture, child abuse, rape, murder, substance abuse, environmental irresponsibility, and school shootings. The vast majority of suffering in this world is the direct result of human sin. And sin is not just the bad things we *do* but also the good things we *don't* do. For example, if we obeyed God's command to put more time, energy, and money into reducing world poverty, suffering would dramatically decrease. Human sin, both the bad things we do and the good things we don't do, causes incredible suffering.

The laws of nature also cause suffering. In order to have life on our planet, natural laws are required. However, those life-giving laws make suffering inevitable. Take gravity, for example. Life could not exist on earth without gravity. But visit the orthopedic wing of any hospital, and you'll learn that gravity sometimes hurts people. Just yesterday at the hospital I visited an elderly woman who fell and broke her hip. Although gravity is a life-giving necessity for life to exist, it also causes pain. The same is true with weather patterns. For example, the collision of warm and cold fronts in the atmosphere that produces life-giving rain also creates occasional tornadoes. On a larger scale, earthquakes and tsunamis sometimes cause enormous suffering in our world, as we saw in the 2004 Indonesian Tsunami and the 2010 Haitian and Chilean earthquakes. Both tsunamis and earthquakes are caused by shifts in the crust of the earth. Our planet could not support life without such shifting. The floating plates of the earth's crust ride on top of molten lava and have to slip past one another, or the planet would disintegrate. Like gravity, the shifting crust of the earth is a life-giving necessity, but it also causes suffering. In short, life as we know it on this planet *cannot exist without pain*. Suffering is the price tag we pay for the glorious gift of being alive.

Human sin and life-giving laws of nature explain much of the suffering in our world but not all of it. Through the years other answers have been offered to explain suffering. For example, some people say that God allows suffering to make us better people and help us grow. Others argue that suffering is caused by demonic forces of evil beyond human sin. Still others remind us that one day all suffering will come to an end. In the final kingdom of God, pain, tears, cancer, war, crime, hurricanes, and terrorism will be forever banned.

All of these answers are tentative and incomplete. No final, definitive answer exists for the problem of suffering. Paul was right: "We know in part" and "We see through the glass dimly." And even if we had perfect answers, would that really help? For example, if Job had received a final, intellectually satisfying reason for all his suffering, it wouldn't change a thing. He would still have open sores all over his body. He would still have ten empty chairs around the table where his children used to sit. An intellectual answer explaining why he was suffering would not heal his body or ease his grief. When suffering occurs, we cannot help but ask, "Why does God allow suffering?" But even if we had an answer, our pain would persist. Therefore a more helpful question might be, "Where is God when suffering occurs?"

Where Is God When It Hurts?

When children get leukemia, teenagers die in accidents, good Christian people contract Lou Gehrig's disease, or communities are devastated by tornadoes, where is God?

That's a profoundly important question. The Christian answer to that question is clear. There's no ambiguity here, no "seeing through the glass dimly." Instead the answer is straightforward. Where is God in the midst of suffering? God is right smack in the middle of it. We learn that from the cross of Jesus.

Several years ago I taught a confirmation classes for our sixth graders on the topic of worship. Just for fun I sent the young people on a scavenger hunt in the sanctuary. I asked them questions like these: How many pews do we have? What hymn is found on page 261? How many black keys are on the piano? What can the choir see that the congregation cannot see? One kid said, "The bald spot on the back of the pastor's head!"

One of the questions was, How many crosses can you find in the sanctuary? The day before, I walked into the sanctuary and counted a processional cross, two crosses on our banners, three on the paraments, one in the stained-glass window, and another one in front of the stained-glass window—for a total of eight crosses. But I was wrong. One child found a cross on the baptismal font, another found one on the top of the Christian flag. One smart sixth grader found even more. He said, "I'm not sure of the exact number, but I estimate there are six hundred crosses in the sanctuary." At first we thought he was crazy, but then he held up a hymnal. On the front cover of every hymnal is a cross. A few moments later, another child held up an offering envelope from a pew rack. She said, "If you add the crosses on our offering envelopes, we have *thousands* of crosses in the sanctuary!" And that's as it should be. Christianity is a religion of the cross. The cross is at the center of our faith.

It's profoundly important for people of faith to remember that we serve a crucified God. The older I get, the more important that becomes to me. Through the years I've prayed with hundreds of cancer patients, preached a lot of hard funerals, counseled with large numbers of broken families, and responded to more tragedies than I care to remember. Like you, I've seen plenty of darkness and suffering in the world. But the cross of Jesus Christ tells us that God is present in the midst of suffering. Good Friday affirms that God enters human suffering, works to relieve suffering, and will ultimately redeem suffering. The cross of Jesus Christ tells us that even in suffering—*especially* in suffering—God is present.

Several years ago I received a phone call from a young couple in my congregation. They called from the neonatal intensive care unit at Vanderbilt Children's Hospital, where I had already made two visits. After three days of valiant effort to save their premature son, the doctors told them he was not going to make it. The parents made the painful decision to remove life-support systems and then asked me to come and baptize their child before he died. When I arrived at the neonatal ICU room, the child's parents, grandmother, nurse, and social worker were waiting for me. In thirty years of ministry, I cannot remember a sadder occasion. And yet, even in that awful setting, God's presence was palpable. We experienced God's presence as we listened to the words of Jesus, "Let the little children come to me" (Matthew 19:14 NIV), and as we recited the promise of Psalm 23, "Yea, though I walk through the valley of the shadow of death, I will fear no evil, for thou art with me" (v. 4 KJV). We knew God was with us as we prayed, "Our Father, who art in heaven. . . ."

We felt the presence of Jesus among us as we blessed the water, baptized the child, anointed him with oil, and commended his spirit to God. Even in overwhelming grief and pain, God's presence permeated the room. As we held one another and cried, we knew that the crucified God was holding us in loving arms and cried with us. We were not alone.

The Crucified God

The cross of Jesus tells us that God is a crucified God. Although God does not take away our suffering, God enters into our pain, shares it with us, and ultimately redeems it — as we will see in Christ's resurrection. The Bible tells us that Jesus is "a man of sorrows, and acquainted with grief" (foretold in Isaiah 53:3 KJV). Jesus' death tells us that when we suffer, God suffers with us.

That was true for a man named David. Twelve years ago David's fourteen-year-old son Rob died in a tragic accident. Several days after the funeral, David, in agonizing grief, drove to a Roman Catholic bookstore. There he purchased a wooden crucifix, depicting Jesus suffering on the cross. David drove home, opened his toolbox, and grabbed a hammer and nail. He then walked to the kitchen and hammered the crucifix to the wall, right above his son's empty chair at the dinner table. Every evening, when he stared at Rob's empty chair, David lifted his eyes to the crucifix and remembered that God, like him, had suffered great grief. The crucifix did not explain his son's death. Nor did it take away the pain of that death. But knowing that God suffered *with* him allowed David to survive that horrible time of pain and grief. Twelve years later that crucifix still hangs on David's wall. It reminds him that the God of the cross is always with him, even in his deepest suffering.

❈ ❈ ❈

Bottom line: *Although God does not prevent suffering, the crucified God fully enters human suffering and works to redeem that suffering.*

CHAPTER 17

❧❧❧

JESUS' RESURRECTION

Is There Hope?

I know that you are looking for Jesus who was crucified. He is not here; for he has been raised.

—the angel, in Matthew 28:5–6

Although I like almost all of Tom Hanks's movies, one of my favorites is *Cast Away*. Hanks received an Academy Award nomination for his powerful role in that film. If you've not seen *Cast Away*, it's a contemporary Robinson Crusoe story. In the movie Tom Hanks plays a FedEx trainer named Chuck Noland. Early in the film, Chuck and several of his colleagues crash into the sea in a company plane crash, killing everyone except Noland. The next day his life raft washes ashore on a deserted island, along with numerous FedEx packages from the airplane. Noland opens the packages, hoping to find items that would help him survive on the island. One box contains a pair of ice skates. Although you wouldn't think ice skates would be much help on a deserted tropical island, Noland manages to find creative uses for them. He uses the shoelaces for rope and one of the ice blades for a hatchet. He even uses one of the skates as a dental tool. I'll spare you the gory details. But you don't ever want to hire Tom Hanks as your dentist!

Noland also finds a package containing a volleyball, which becomes his one and only friend, "Wilson." Another box contains videotapes, which Noland uses as rope. One of the boxes Noland finds on the beach has angel wings on the outside, but interestingly, he never opens it. Instead, Noland saves that package the entire four years he lives on the island. When he finally departs the island on a raft, he lashes the unopened package onto his boat and takes it with him.

"This Package Saved My Life"

In the final scene of the movie, Noland, now safely back in the United States, drives down a lonely Texas highway with the unopened angel wings FedEx package in the passenger seat of his car. As he drives, you can hear his radio playing Elvis's old song "Return to Sender," which is exactly what Noland is doing. He is returning the package to its original sender in rural Texas. He finally arrives at the house and knocks on the door, but nobody is home. Noland places the box at the front door along with a note that says, "This package saved my life." A few minutes later the movie ends.

So what did Chuck Noland mean when he wrote, "This package saved my life"? He never opened it. He didn't use its contents. Yet he claims it saved his life. If you've seen the movie, it's obvious what he meant. That package symbolized hope for Chuck Noland. It represented his hope that one day he would leave that island, go home to family and friends, return to his job—and deliver that package. It was, quite literally, a package of hope. And that hope kept him going for four hard years on a deserted island. At one point the endless drudgery and overwhelming loneliness of the island almost drove him to suicide. But hope of returning home kept him from doing so. "This package saved my life," said Noland. But what he really meant was "Hope saved my life."

I've been in the people business for over thirty years now. One thing I've learned during these years is that hope saves people's lives. Hope saves them spiritually, emotionally, relationally, and sometimes even physically. People hope for many things. They hope for forgiveness, reconciliation, and healing. They hope that faith will return, finances will recover, or grief will finally end. They hope that their addiction can be overcome or their marriage can be saved. They hope for life beyond divorce or courage to face "the valley of the shadow of death." When people can keep hope alive, they somehow find the strength to take another step in spite of the darkness and pain of the present moment. Hope is a powerful force. Hope can save a person's life in every way a life can be saved. And hope is what the resurrection of Jesus Christ is all about.

Sunday's Coming

Little hope remained for the followers of Christ on Good Friday and on Saturday. They saw their beloved Jesus betrayed, abandoned, placed on trial, mocked, beaten, and crucified. They watched as his abused, lifeless body was placed in a tomb. The disciples of Jesus felt utterly devastated; all hope vanished. They hid from the authorities, fearful for their own lives. But on the third day, on Easter Sunday, God declared that death would not prevail and evil would not win.

Early on Easter morning, the incredible news broke forth, "He is not here; he has risen!" (Luke 24:6 NIV).

And that news of Christ's resurrection from the grave gave Jesus' followers renewed hope—hope for life and hope even for death. The last word of the gospel is not crucifixion but resurrection. The last word of the gospel is not despair but hope. The resurrection of Jesus Christ tells us that God is in the business of bringing life out of death. And God doesn't just bring life out of physical death, important as that is. God also brings life out of smaller deaths, like the death of a dream, the death of a marriage, the death of a career, or the death of good health. And that great Easter hope—that God brings life out of death—gives us hope for living and even hope for dying.

Christianity stands or falls on the resurrection of Jesus Christ. As the apostle Paul says in 1 Corinthians 15, "If there is no resurrection of the dead, then Christ has not been raised; and if Christ has not been raised, then our proclamation has been in vain and your faith has been in vain" (vv. 13–14). But our faith is *not* in vain. Paul continues, "But in fact Christ has been raised from the dead, the first fruits of those who have died" (v. 20). Therefore, Paul concludes, "Death has been swallowed up in victory. Where, O death, is your victory? Where, O death, is your sting? . . . But thanks be to God, who gives us the victory through our Lord Jesus Christ" (vv. 54–55, 57).

"And When I Die, Give Me Jesus"

Several months ago I ate lunch with my close friend and fellow United Methodist minister Michael Welch. During lunch we talked shop, laughed, and fussed a bit about United Methodist bureaucracy. Mostly we enjoyed being together. Michael and I ate lunch together every two weeks for over four years.

One week later, on a miserable, cold, rainy day in middle Tennessee, I attended Michael's funeral. Three days earlier Michael, his wife, and their two young children died in a car wreck. A semitrailer truck rear-ended their van, instantly killing all four of them.

I went to the funeral early, hoping to find a seat in the little country church where Michael served as pastor. Before the service began, I walked to the front of the sanctuary. Pictures of the family sat on a table, along with artwork and personal items belonging to the children. As I looked at the photographs and personal effects of the family, the enormity of that loss hit me. I've officiated at some hard funerals in my life. But I've never buried an entire family. As I took my seat, tears rolling down my cheeks, I thought to myself, *Nothing can redeem this awful tragedy.*

A half hour later the service began. A woman from the choir walked to the pulpit and began to sing a song I'd never heard before. I later learned that it was an old hymn, but it was new to me. The song—slow, sad, and sweet— felt appropriate for the occasion. She began to sing, "And when I die, give me Jesus."

As I sat in the pew and listened to the song, it dawned on me: the only thing that could begin to redeem this nightmare was Jesus. The only thing that offered any hope was that Michael and his family loved, served, and belonged to Jesus Christ, "the resurrection and the life." Michael lived and died by that hope, hope rooted in Jesus' victory over the grave. Christ's resurrection did not answer the question of why Michael and his family died. Nor did it take away the pain and grief we all felt. But the resurrection of Jesus Christ offered hope that death was not the final word for Michael, Julie, Jesse, and Hannah Welch.

As a Christian minister I officiate at a lot of funerals. Each funeral service is unique, depending on the person who died. However, one part of the liturgy never changes. I begin every funeral for a Christian believer with the words of Jesus, "I am the resurrection and the life. Those who believe in me, even though they die, will live" (John 11:25). In life, in death, and in life beyond death, we are hopeful people because of the resurrection of Jesus Christ our Lord. Thanks be to God!

The Last Word Is Hope

My all-time favorite movie is *The Shawshank Redemption*, starring Tim Robbins and Morgan Freeman. *The Shawshank Redemption* tells the story of a young bank executive named Andy Dufresne. Andy, falsely convicted of murdering his wife and her lover, is sentenced to two life terms in a notoriously brutal state penitentiary called Shawshank Prison. While there he meets a man named Red, and the two strike up a unique friendship. It's a long and complex story, but ultimately it's a story about affirming hope in a place where little hope exists.

In spite of being an innocent man in a tough prison, Andy holds on to hope—hope of escape, and hope of life beyond prison walls. And that hope is what keeps him going. Andy's dream is to go to a little Mexican town on the Pacific Ocean called Zihuatanejo. His plans include buying and running a hotel, including fixing up an old boat to take his guests deep-sea fishing. He once asks Red to be his assistant, but Red says he doesn't think he can make it in the outside world. A few minutes later Red chastises Andy for holding on to such a fairly-tale pipedream.

In one of many powerful scenes in the movie, Andy talks with his friends about the need for hope, especially in prison. Red, angered by Andy's naive words of hope, says, "Let me tell you something, Andy Dufresne. Hope is a dangerous thing. Hope can drive a man insane. It's got no use on the inside [of prison]."

But Andy doesn't buy what Red has said. Andy continues to hope, even after twenty hard years at Shawshank prison. And Andy doesn't just have hope for himself: he also inspires hope in others. For example, he helps young men get their GED, and he builds a first-class library for the inmates. In the end Andy even inspires hope in his dear friend Red, the one who has said, "Hope is a dangerous thing."

After spending twenty years in Shawshank prison for a crime he did not commit, Andy finally escapes. Not long after Andy's escape, Red finds himself paroled. But Red isn't adjusting well to life outside prison. In fact, he almost decides to commit a crime so he can return to the security of prison life. However, one thing keeps him from implementing that plan. Andy has left Red a letter, inviting him to come to Zihuatanejo and be his helper at his hotel. In the letter Andy says to Red, "Remember, hope is a good thing, maybe the best of things, and no good thing ever dies." And so, with hope in his heart, Red decides to go to Mexico. As he travels on the bus, excited as a schoolboy, Red speaks the final words of the movie: "I hope I can make it across the border. I hope to see my friend and shake his hand. I hope the Pacific is as blue as it has been in my dreams. I hope."

Like the gospel of Jesus Christ, the final word of *The Shawshank Redemption* is the word *hope*. In the final scene of the movie, Red and Andy are reunited on the beach at Zihuatanejo. And so it happens that through the power of hope, Red is finally redeemed.

✧   ✧   ✧

Bottom line: *Jesus Christ's resurrection gives us hope for life and even hope for death.*

CHAPTER 18

─── ✿ ───

JESUS' LEGACY

Is the Church Still Relevant?

On this rock I will build my church, and the gates of Hades will not prevail against it.

—Jesus, in Matthew 16:18

Once I heard about a businessman from up north who came down south for a conference in Durham, North Carolina. His first morning in town, he went to eat breakfast at a little mom-and-pop diner close to his hotel. The waitress came to take his order. He ordered eggs, sausage, and toast. When the waitress, a Southerner, brought this Northerner his order, he noticed a pile of white stuff on his plate. "What's that?" he asked.

"Grits," she said.

"What is a grit?" he asked.

"Honey," she drawled in her Southern accent, "they don't come by themselves."

Grits don't come by themselves, and neither do Christians. The Christian faith is not an individualistic faith but a community faith. Followers of Christ need a community of faith to worship God, serve their community, love and support one another, ask hard questions, grow and learn, laugh and cry, experience healing, navigate ethics, seek transcendence, affirm faith and hope, and find strength for the journey. Christians "don't come by themselves." Instead, they come in communities. As a pastor, I constantly see the benefits of belonging to a church family, as a recent weekend at my congregation vividly reminded me.

A Busy Weekend at First Church

Several months ago on a Friday night, I led a wedding rehearsal for a lifelong member of our congregation. Immediately before the rehearsal began, word came that a beloved matriarch of our church had just died after a long battle with cancer. As soon as we completed the wedding rehearsal, our associate pastor and I went to see the family. We talked with them about their wife/mother/grandmother, alternating between laughter and tears. Before we left, we served Holy Communion to the family. It served as a powerful reminder that God's presence would sustain them during this tough time. After receiving the elements of Communion, we anointed them with oil on their foreheads in the sign of the cross, praying that God's comforting grace would help them through their grief.

The next evening, on Saturday night, the congregation gathered in the sanctuary to celebrate the wedding of one of our children. Twenty-five years earlier, when she was just an infant, the congregation had witnessed her baptism. Through that baptism God initiated her into the life of the church. During the baptism her parents, along with the congregation, made a sacred vow to raise her in the love and nurture of Jesus and his church. For the next twenty-five years our church lived out that vow.

They rocked, held, and loved her in the nursery. They taught her about the love of Jesus in Sunday school. They told her the stories of the Bible at summer camp and vacation Bible school. They taught her to sing "Jesus loves me, this I know" in children's choir. They educated her about the great doctrines of the faith in confirmation classes. They put up with her annoying adolescent attitude during her teenage years in the youth group. They sent her cards and cookies while she attended college. When she came home from college, they began a new Sunday school class for her and other young adults her age. And, for twenty-five years, they helped her connect to God through weekly worship. So with great joy, laughter, and a few tears, they watched her exchange sacred marriage vows with her husband at the same altar where they baptized her twenty-five years earlier. Then they threw her a glorious and joyful party at the reception that followed.

The next morning our congregation gathered for Sunday school and worship. During Sunday school good friends shared joys and concerns. They prayed together, laughed together, and a few even cried together. After that they studied a biblical or theological lesson and discussed some aspect of what it means to be a Christian believer in the twenty-first century. During worship the early crowd sang praise choruses to the beat of drums and guitars, while the late crowd sang hymns accompanied by the organ. Both groups greeted one another in Christian love with handshakes and hugs during the passing of the peace. They prayed the Lord's Prayer, affirmed their faith, and listened to Scripture. And they heard a sermon on God's grace and celebrated God's mysterious presence at Holy Communion. After the benediction and a final song, they left the sanctuary, talking to one another with great affection as they departed.

That afternoon at 2:00 p.m., many of our members gathered back in the sanctuary for the funeral of the matriarch mentioned above. As we remembered and celebrated her life, we sang, laughed, and cried. Mostly we affirmed hope that she belonged to Jesus Christ, "the resurrection and the life." We ended the service with her favorite hymn and then recited the ancient words of the Apostles' Creed, including "I believe in the resurrection of the body and the life everlasting."

Later that Sunday evening the congregation gathered once again for our "Fantastically Fun Follies" in the Family Life Center. After eating a bountiful potluck dinner together, we enjoyed a talent show from the congregation. The talents included everything from a precious five-year-old girl singing "Tomorrow," to a senior adult woman telling a tall tale, to a middle-age Sunday school class singing "On the Boardwalk," complete with sunglasses and dance steps. Throughout the show people clapped liberally, and laughter filled the room. After a final prayer we departed, looking forward to seeing one another again the following Sunday.

When I arrived home that Sunday night and reflected on the weekend, three things came to mind. First, I felt utterly exhausted! Thankfully, not every weekend is that busy. Second, I felt an overwhelming sense of gratitude and joy to be a pastor. And finally, I asked myself, *How do people live without a community of faith?*

"I Will Build My Church"

During his public ministry, Jesus engaged in many activities, including preaching, teaching, and healing. However, nothing mattered more to Jesus than establishing his church. In Matthew 16, Jesus says to his disciples, "I will build my church, and the gates of Hades will not prevail against it" (v. 18). Matthew also tells us that before his ascension, Jesus commissioned his church to carry on his mission: "All authority in heaven and on earth has been given to me. Go therefore and make disciples of all nations, baptizing them in the name of the Father and of the Son and of the Holy Spirit, and teaching them to obey everything that I have commanded you. And remember, I am with you always, to the end of the age" (28:18–20).

For over two thousand years, the church has carried on Jesus' mission to the world. We continue to teach and preach the gospel, heal the sick, care for the poor, lift up the discouraged, and seek God's kingdom "on earth as it is in heaven." Although flawed, we are still the people of God, representing Christ to others.

The church of Jesus Christ has blessed my life beyond measure. Everything I am, I owe to God and God's church. So when I talk about the church, I do so with love, enthusiasm, and devotion. However, that does not mean I don't get frustrated with the church. I most certainly do! Churches and their members, me included, can sometimes be petty, hypocritical, judgmental, resistant to change, and self-absorbed. In spite of my great love for Christ's church, I can sometimes relate to this old, worn-out story that preachers still love to tell.

Early one Sunday morning a woman woke up her husband. "Honey," she said, "You need to get up and get ready for church." He promptly rolled over and went back to sleep. Ten minutes later she came back into the bedroom and said, "You have to get up, or you'll be late for church." Once again he fell back asleep. Finally she came into the bedroom for a third time. With voice raised she said, "Get out of that bed right now and get ready for church!"

The man, now awake and irritated, replied, "I don't want to go to church. It's boring. It's full of hypocrites. And the people there don't care about me one bit. In fact, I'm absolutely fed up with that church! You give me one good reason why I should get out of this bed and go to church."

His wife replied, "I'll give you a good reason. You're the pastor of that church, and you *have* to go."

Most pastors and laypeople can relate to that story. We love our church, but sometimes we get frustrated with it. And yet, in spite of its many flaws, God still loves the church and uses it as God's primary vehicle for working in the world.

Being Church in a Tough Place

Years ago I served as the pastor of West Helena Baptist Church. During my tenure at that church, the local economy collapsed. Thousands of good jobs left the community, and people moved away in droves. Businesses closed down, housing values plummeted, and unemployment went through the roof. In addition, race relations were severely strained, the public-school system was in chaos, and the local government was close to bankruptcy.

Every church in the community, mine included, was hemorrhaging members, money, and morale. I seemed to spend all my time saying good-bye to families who were moving away or burying those who stayed. In that context people naturally felt anxious and angry. All that local negativity and conflict made its way into the churches of the community, including West Helena Baptist Church.

One Monday morning, a few minutes after the mail arrived, our financial secretary began laughing uncontrollably. She finally caught her breath and shouted,

"Everyone come here!" The entire staff rushed to her office. Still laughing, she handed me an envelope. She said, "Look at the name of the church on the front of the envelope." You need to remember, I was serving at *West Helena* Baptist Church. But the envelope was addressed to *West Hell* Baptist Church. The financial secretary said, "It's bad enough to live in hell, but to live in west hell — that's really the pits!"

From that day on, the staff lovingly referred to our church as the "West Hell" Baptist Church. And "West Hell" proved to be a tough place to serve. However, the congregation included many wonderful and loving folks. And in spite of the massive community struggles, God continued to work in that church. People's lives were changed, people found hope for their journey, people encountered God in worship, and significant ministry was done in the name of Christ. The Spirit of God was still alive and well, even at the "West Hell" Baptist Church.

When I think of the church, I often remember West Helena. Every church, even the best of them, has struggles and flaws. The church is never all it should be. It never fully lives up to its ideals. And it never has, not even in the beginning. The Bible is refreshingly honest about the inadequacies of the early church. Although we often romanticize and idealize the New Testament church, it had massive problems. The early church consisted of imperfect people, just like today's church. But God loved and used the early church for God's purposes and continues to do so today.

Jesus' great legacy is the Christian church. For all its weakness, the church is still a place to discover God's presence, grace, and strength for the journey. The church, in spite of its failures, is still the beloved bride of Christ. In spite of its flaws, the church still has a great mission and is still God's primary way of doing business in the world.

When we live up to our ideals and even when we don't, Jesus loves his church. We would do well to follow his example.

❈ ❈ ❈

Bottom line: *In spite of its flaws, the church is still God's primary vehicle for doing God's work in the world, and every Christian needs to belong to one.*

CHAPTER 19

∽⁓∽

JESUS' PROMISE

Who Is the Holy Spirit?

The Advocate, the Holy Spirit, whom the Father will send in my name, will teach you everything, and remind you of all that I have said to you.

—Jesus, in John 14:26

Several months ago one of my in-laws called me on the phone at ten o'clock on Saturday night. He said, "Tomorrow morning my Sunday school class is discussing the Trinity. But I just don't get it. Can you explain the Trinity to me in three minutes or less? And while you're at it, will you also explain the Holy Spirit."

I laughed so hard I almost cried. Why? Because the church has been trying to understand and explain the Trinity and the Holy Spirit for two thousand years. There is no three-minute explanation!

Like my relative, when it comes to the Trinity and the Holy Spirit, a lot of Christians "just don't get it." In spite of millions of sermons, books, lectures, confirmation and

Sunday school classes, the theology of the Trinity and the Holy Spirit remains vague for many believers. Obviously, one short chapter will not resolve that. However, a few comments are in order.

The Trinity in Three Minutes

Although the doctrine of the Trinity is not neatly spelled out in the Bible, we do catch glimpses of Trinitarian theology in the New Testament. For example, at Jesus' baptism, God the Father, Son, and Holy Spirit are all referenced. God the Son seeks baptism in the river Jordan from John the Baptist. When Jesus comes out of the water, God the Holy Spirit descends on him like a dove. Then God the Father says, "This is my Son, whom I love; with him I am well pleased" (Matthew 3:17 NIV). Although this passage does not constitute a clear theology of the Trinity, it does offer an *image* of the Trinity. The same thing can be seen in the Great Commission of Matthew 28. In this passage, Jesus commands his disciples to "go therefore and make disciples of all nations, baptizing them *in the name of the Father and of the Son and of the Holy Spirit*" (v. 19, with added emphasis). Although Trinitarian theology is not comprehensively mapped out in this baptismal formula, the early church clearly had a Trinitarian concept.

The doctrine of the Trinity grew out of the experience of the early church. Rooted in Jewish faith, early Christian believers clearly understood God as Father and Creator. That was the theological water in which they swam. But then they encountered Jesus of Nazareth. Never before had they met anyone like Jesus. His teachings and miracles overwhelmed them. Clearly God empowered this man in a unique and mysterious way. Before long they began to realize that Jesus wasn't just close to God: in some way

Jesus *was* God. As we saw earlier in chapter 11, the apostle Peter once proclaimed, "You are the Christ, the Son of the living God" (Matthew 16:16 NIV). Jesus' friend Martha makes a similar affirmation in John 11 when she says, "I believe that you are the Messiah, the Son of God" (v. 27). In John 14, Jesus says, "Whoever has seen me has seen the Father" (v. 9). In short, the early followers of Jesus experienced God both as God the Father and God the Son.

Following his death and resurrection, Jesus departed this world. But God's presence did not leave the church. Even though Jesus was physically gone, the early church continued to experience his presence among them. They understood this presence to be God the Holy Spirit. Before leaving them, Jesus in John 14 promises the disciples, "I will ask the Father, and he will give you another Advocate, to be with you forever" (v. 16). Jesus continues, "The Advocate, the Holy Spirit, whom the Father will send in my name, will teach you everything, and remind you of all that I have said to you" (v. 26). The doctrine of the Trinity grew out of the direct experience of the early church. They experienced God as Father, Son, and Holy Spirit. Eventually this experiential reality of God became the formal doctrine of the Trinity, God in three persons — Father, Son, and Holy Spirit.

Although all analogies break down, perhaps this one will help you better understand the Trinity. I know a medical doctor named Mary Jackson. During the day, Mary's patients experience her as "Dr. Jackson." A skilled and competent doctor, she relates to her patients in a kind yet professional manner. Mary is the mother of two young girls, Jennifer and Elizabeth. When Mary greets her children after school, they jump on her, hug her, and the three of them laugh and wrestle. Mary's children don't call her "Dr. Jackson": they call her "Mommy." Mary is married to a banker named Larry. He does not experience Mary as "Dr. Jackson" or "Mommy." Instead, Larry relates to Mary as wife, friend, and lover. Mary is one person, not three. However, she is experienced in three distinct ways—as doctor, mother, and wife. In the same way God is one entity, not three. However, we experience God in three ways—as God the Father, God the Son, and God the Holy Spirit. If you don't push that analogy too far, it might be helpful. It's the best "three-minute explanation" of the Trinity I can offer!

Slain in the Spirit

Before Jesus ascended into heaven, he promised his followers that God the Father would send the Holy Spirit to be with them forever. So let's look further at Jesus' promise and ask the question "Who is the Holy Spirit?"

When I first became a Christian in a Baptist church at age fifteen, I enthusiastically participated in all congregational activities. But about a year later, in my adolescent idealism, I began to think, *This church is dead*. For example, our Sunday morning worship services felt lifeless. I couldn't understand that. On Friday nights members of my church went to football games and screamed their lungs out. On Saturday nights they went to the movies and laughed or cried their hearts out. But on Sunday morning when they gathered in church, they didn't scream or laugh or cry: they slept! That lack of vitality, energy, and joy at our worship services deeply frustrated me.

About that time, a friend invited me to his church, an Assembly of God congregation. Back then we called them Holy Roller churches. My friend called it a "Holy-Spirit-filled church." That sounded good to me so I went for a visit. I'll never forget my first Sunday at that church. They started out with a song. As they sang, everybody raised their hands into the air. Although it felt uncomfortable, I managed to raise my hands slightly. After they sang, the preacher said, "Let us pray." I expected the preacher to say the prayer, so what happened next blew me away. All of a sudden every person in the church started praying out loud. I nearly jumped out of my skin! Next came the Scripture reading. During the reading a man behind me shouted at the top of his lungs, "Hallelujah!" Nobody at my church ever said "hallelujah" unless it was printed in the bulletin—and then only meekly. Next the preacher began his sermon. He preached like he had consumed ten cups of cappuccino during Sunday school! His sermon was all about being "slain in the Spirit." When he finished preaching, the congregation started singing the invitation song. As they sang, people walked forward to get slain in the Spirit. The preacher put his hands on their heads, shouted things about Jesus and the Holy Spirit, and then they fell backward. Ushers caught them as they fell so they wouldn't hurt themselves.

I didn't understand what was going on, but I knew I didn't want be slain in the Spirit. In fact, I wished I was back in the Baptist church sleeping! After folks got slain in the Spirit, they started speaking in tongues. Finally they had a healing service. Over two hours later the service finally ended. Although the experience unnerved me, their emphasis on the Holy Spirit intrigued me. I went back that evening and again on Wednesday night. For several months I went to that church every Sunday morning, Sunday evening, and Wednesday night. I also went to a couple of revival meetings.

In fact, I got in trouble a few times for going. I would get home about eleven on a school night, and my mom would ask me, "Where have you been?"

I told her, "I've been to church."

"Right," she said, "where have you *really* been?" My mom didn't understand the Pentecostal Church. She obviously had not been slain in the Spirit!

About five months later, during another revival meeting, I had an epiphany. I realized that the Pentecostal church I was attending didn't have any more Holy Spirit in it than the Baptist church I belonged to. The Pentecostal church was certainly *different* than the Baptist church. It was far more emotionally expressive, and its worship style was radically different. But the same Holy Spirit could be found at both places. They just experienced the Spirit in different ways. So I decided to return to my own Baptist church, where they slept on Sunday mornings. Years later I became a United Methodist. And Methodists don't just sleep in church: they slip right into a coma!

Although I've never returned to the Pentecostal church and would not be comfortable there today, I'm grateful for that experience and have great appreciation for their tradition. I'm especially grateful for their emphasis on the Holy Spirit. I don't agree with some of their teachings about the Holy Spirit. For example, I don't believe you have to speak in tongues to be filled with the Spirit. But I do appreciate their emphasis on the Spirit. By and large, mainline churches neglect the Holy Spirit. We seem uncomfortable talking about the Spirit. Our discomfort with the Holy Spirit reminds me of a story about a layman named Tom.

One Monday morning Tom went to visit his pastor. He said, "Pastor, I've been filled with the Holy Spirit."

His pastor said, "What do you mean you've been filled with the Spirit?"

Tom said, "I went to the Holy Spirit Tabernacle of God Church last night and got filled with the Spirit."

His pastor replied, "Tom, you can't be filled with the Spirit. You're a Lutheran."

"I Believe in the Holy Spirit"

Every Sunday, thousands of mainline churches recite the Apostles' Creed, including the words "I believe in the Holy Spirit." But what does that really mean? Before trying to answer that question further, a disclaimer is in order. We will never fully understand the Holy Spirit. There's great mystery in this doctrine—as there should be. In John 3, Jesus compares the Holy Spirit to the wind: "The wind blows wherever it pleases. You hear its sound, but you cannot tell where it comes from or where it is going. So it is with everyone born of the Spirit" (v. 8 NIV). In other words, says Jesus, you cannot nail down the Holy Spirit. You cannot figure out a clear-cut doctrine of the Holy Spirit and write it down in a neat formula. When we talk about the Holy Spirit, we must leave room for ambiguity, uncertainty, and mystery.

However, on the other hand, there is much we *do* know about the Holy Spirit. The Bible, Christian history, and Christian theology have much to teach us about the Spirit. When you boil it all down, the basic teaching of Scripture and Christian theology is this: the Holy Spirit is *God's empowering presence.*

God's Empowering Presence

As mentioned earlier in this chapter, after Jesus' departure, the early church was vividly aware of Christ's ongoing divine presence in their midst. They came to understand that presence as God the Holy Spirit. That same empowering presence of God is alive and well today. Let me give you three examples.

1. *God's empowering presence can be found in the church.* Everything the church does, it does in the power of the

Holy Spirit. A vivid example is congregational worship. When God's church gathers for worship, the Holy Spirit gathers with us. As we sing, pray, read Scripture, proclaim the gospel, baptize, and celebrate Holy Communion, God's empowering presence is, in the words of a popular praise song, "In this very room." The Holy Spirit is also with God's church in our evangelism efforts, education programs, community ministries, and fellowship.

2. *God's empowering presence can be found in individual Christians.* Christian believers are constantly empowered by God's Holy Spirit. For example, the Spirit gives us guidance as we struggle with important decisions. The Spirit helps us cope with difficult circumstances. The Spirit helps us live lives of integrity. The Spirit helps us share our faith with others. The Spirit helps us forgive people who hurt us. The Spirit helps us serve others. The Spirit helps us pray, even when our words are inadequate. The Spirit helps us grow and mature in our faith. The Spirit gives us hope even in the midst of illness, divorce, or death. The Spirit comforts us in losses. The Spirit helps us develop Christian traits of love, joy, peace, patience, kindness, goodness, faithfulness, gentleness, and self-control—what the Bible calls the "fruit of the Spirit." Finally, the Spirit gives Christian believers spiritual abilities and gifts that we can use to serve God and others.

3. *God's empowering presence can be found in the world.* The same Holy Spirit that works in individual Christians and in the church also works on a global scale. For example, when the gospel is proclaimed around the world, the Holy Spirit is at work. When caring ministry is done throughout the nations in the name of Jesus, the Holy Spirit is at work. When the Berlin wall was torn down and South Africa's apartheid collapsed, the Holy Spirit was at work. When peace efforts are made in the Middle East and other troubled places, the Holy Spirit is at work. When medical

breakthroughs are made in medicine, such as improved treatments for cancer, diabetes, or AIDS, the Holy Spirit is at work. When efforts are made to vanquish racism, poverty, ignorance, or injustice, the Holy Spirit is at work. For those with eyes to see, the Holy Spirit—God's empowering presence—can be found everywhere: in the church, in individual lives, and throughout the world.

❉ ❉ ❉

Bottom line: *The Holy Spirit is God's empowering presence in our lives, in the life of the church, and in the world.*

CHAPTER 20

❧

JESUS' VISION

What Is God's Dream for the World?

Your kingdom come. Your will be done, on earth as it is in heaven.
—Jesus, teaching the Lord's Prayer in Matthew 6:10

One of the perks of my job is receiving pictures from children in the congregation. Fairly often on Sunday mornings, a child hands me a picture he or she drew during the service. For example, a few weeks ago after the early worship service, a little girl gave me a hug and then handed me a picture she drew during the service. The picture depicted me standing in front of the congregation, preaching a sermon. At the bottom of the picture she wrote, "You are a great pastor to have. I love you, Pastor Martin." I save these pictures in a file in my office. They are among my most valuable possessions.

Several months ago I preached a sermon on the kingdom of God. After worship a boy in the congregation handed me a picture of a big castle. At the top of the castle were the words "God's Kingdom," and under that, "Jesus' Kingdom." He drew a heart in the middle of the castle, depicting God's love. At the bottom of the picture he printed, GOD AND JESUS RULE! Although this boy is only nine years old, he already has a good understanding of God's kingdom. The kingdom of God is what the world would look like if God ruled the world.

"Thy Kingdom Come"

When Jesus first arrives on the public scene, he proclaims the coming kingdom of God. Matthew tells the story: immediately following his baptism and temptation in the desert, Jesus begins to preach, "Repent, for the kingdom of heaven is near" (4:17 NIV). Later, in Matthew 6, Jesus teaches his disciples to pray, "Your kingdom come. Your will be done, on earth as it is in heaven" (v. 10). Throughout the Gospels, Jesus constantly preaches and teaches about the kingdom of God. Jesus' primary passion in life, the thing that most motivates him, is God's coming kingdom.

Unfortunately for most Americans, the kingdom of God is a vague and ambiguous concept. Since we live in a democracy, and not under a king or queen, it's difficult for us to think in kingdom terms. However, the ancient world fully understood the concept of kingdom. It meant the absolute rule of a monarch. In a kingdom the king called all the shots. So when Jesus taught his disciples to pray, "Thy kingdom come," he taught them to pray for God's rule in the world. In short, Jesus asked them to pray for a new world order, a world where God ruled.

The kingdom of God is what the world would look like if God's will were done "on earth as it is in heaven." If that were true, wars and terrorism would come to an end;

hunger would be a distant memory; broken relationships would be healed; pollution and global warming would vanish; illnesses would be banned; and love, mercy, and justice would prevail for all.

Sadly, we don't see a lot of God's kingdom in today's world. When we watch the evening news, Brian Williams, Katie Couric, and Diane Sawyer don't say much about God's reign on earth. Instead of God's kingdom, we see terrorist attacks, endless wars, environmental disasters, and people struggling in poverty. Where's the kingdom of God in all that?

I recently heard about a pastor leading his congregation in a Sunday morning prayer for God's kingdom to come. He prayed for peace, justice, compassion, and healing. But then, right in the middle of his prayer, he stopped abruptly and burst out in frustration, "Lord, we bring you these same petitions every week, and it doesn't do any good." That woke up his congregation! But can't you relate? We pray for God's kingdom to come, but the kingdom seems a long way off. As a result, most Christians don't take the kingdom of God seriously. Or if we do, we relegate it to the future. We say, when Jesus returns, *then* we'll see God's kingdom come "on earth as it is in heaven." And there's truth in that. God's kingdom will never fully come until Christ returns and ushers in a new age.

But Jesus didn't say the kingdom was just for the future. He said, "The kingdom of God has come near," and "The kingdom of God is among you" (Luke 10:11; 17:21). To be sure, the kingdom is not yet fully realized. Rather, said Jesus, the kingdom of God is like yeast in the dough, slowly causing the bread to rise. Or the kingdom of God is like a tiny mustard seed, quietly growing into a large bush. It's not easily seen. But if we look carefully, we can catch glimpses of the kingdom of God.

Glimpses of the Kingdom

One of the privileges of being a pastor is that I get to see glimpses of the kingdom on a regular basis. For example, I used to pastor in an agricultural community in Arkansas. One year, right at harvesttime, a farmer in town suddenly died, leaving his crops in the field and a wife and three young children at home. I watched farmers from my church, who had crops of their own to bring in, go to that man's farm and work day and night, bringing in the harvest for his wife and children. You could see them in their combines at night, floodlights in the fields, working to bring in a dead man's harvest. Only after they finished harvesting the dead man's crop did they begin to harvest their own crops. For many, it just looked like farmers in the field. But for those with eyes to see, it was a glimpse of the kingdom of God.

In the church I served in Honolulu, a group of members regularly go to the leper colony at Kalaupapa on the island of Molokai. The residents don't have leprosy anymore, but their bodies still carry its scars. Many are missing fingers or hands or have other health problems, and all of them are very old. So members of that Honolulu church go to Kalaupapa once a quarter and do things the residents cannot do for themselves, including detailed housecleaning, painting, auto mechanics, and sewing. They also take hundreds of homemade cookies from the congregation—always a popular item! At the end of the weekend, the members of my old church and the residents at the leper colony gather in their little church and worship God together. It's a simple ministry. But it's also a beautiful glimpse of the kingdom of God.

In the church I served in Mt. Juliet, Tennessee, I saw a glimpse of the kingdom every month at a fish fry. Yes, a fish fry! Our church put on a huge fish dinner the first

Saturday night of every month. At first they used the money to pay the medical bills of a girl in the congregation who was struggling with cancer. However, after she died, the congregation decided to keep having the fish fry, using the money to help low-income people in the community pay their medical expenses. It's just a fish fry, but it's also a glimpse of the kingdom of God.

Jesus tells us the kingdom of God is all around us if we have the eyes to see. The kingdom is not yet fully realized: it's like a mustard seed quietly growing or like yeast slowly rising in the flour. But it's there, working God's purposes in the world. And you and I are invited to be a part of that kingdom. When we pray "Thy kingdom come," we are asking God to let us play a small part in advancing God's kingdom.

Kingdom Living

If we took Jesus' prayer "Thy kingdom come" seriously, it would make dramatic changes in our lives. For example, it would radically impact our marriage and family life. Can you imagine if God ruled in your family, in my family? If so, we would treat one another with love, compassion, and respect. And when we fail one another, we would readily offer grace and forgiveness. If we took this prayer seriously, we would change the way we spend our money. We would keep far less money in our checkbooks and investment accounts and give far more to church and other charitable organizations that support kingdom work locally and around the world. If we took this prayer seriously, we would change the way we use our time. We would spend less time in selfish pursuits and more time helping others. If we took this prayer seriously, we would change the way we do our jobs. We would work with better attitudes and with absolute integrity. If we took this prayer seriously, what a difference it would make in our lives!

Although the kingdom of God impacts people on a personal level, it also has profound social ramifications. A great biblical example can be found in Isaiah 65. In this powerful passage of Scripture, we capture a glimpse of God's dream for the world.

Dreaming God's Dream

In chapter 65 Isaiah says, "Never again will there be in it an infant who lives but a few days" (v. 20 NIV). In God's kingdom, infant mortality does not exist. Therefore, issues like health insurance and prenatal care are kingdom issues. Isaiah then says, "Never again will there be . . . an old man who does not live out his years" (v. 20 NIV). In God's kingdom, senior adults live long, productive, and healthy lives. Therefore, issues like Medicare and Social Security are kingdom issues. Isaiah adds, "They will build houses and dwell in them" (v. 21 NIV). In God's kingdom, every person lives in a decent house. Therefore, issues like fair mortgage rates and affordable housing are kingdom issues. Isaiah continues, "They will plant vineyards and eat their fruit" (v. 21 NIV). In God's kingdom, food is plentiful. Therefore, healthy, accessible, and affordable food is a kingdom issue. Isaiah goes on to say, "[They] will long enjoy the works of their hands. They will not toil in vain" (v. 22–23 NIV). In God's kingdom, people are fairly compensated for their work. Therefore, issues like minimum wage and employee benefits are kingdom issues. Then Isaiah says, "They will not . . . bear children doomed to misfortune" (v. 23 NIV). In God's kingdom, children thrive. Therefore, issues like child nutrition and early education are kingdom issues. Finally, Isaiah dreams of the day when "the wolf and the lamb will feed together, and the lion will eat straw like the ox. . . . They will neither harm nor destroy on all my holy mountain" (v. 25 NIV). In God's kingdom, violence and warfare are contraband. Therefore, peacemaking between peoples and nations is a major kingdom issue.

Because these kinds of social issues matter to God, they should also matter to the people of God. Individual Christians, local churches, denominations, and the entire worldwide church must constantly seek ways to advance God's kingdom, both locally and around the world. Therefore, both in our personal lives and in the broader social world, let us continue to pray for and work toward making Jesus' dream a reality: "Your kingdom come. Your will be done, on earth as it is in heaven."

❊   ❊   ❊

Bottom line: *The kingdom of God is God's dream for the world, and we are called to help make that dream a reality, both in our personal lives and in society.*

CHAPTER 21

⬥

A FINAL QUESTION

*Do Mainline Christians Believe
in Getting Saved?*

For the Son of Man came to seek out and to save the lost.
                                        —Jesus, in Luke 19:10

Not long ago someone asked me, "Do mainline churches believe in getting saved?" The short answer to that question is "Yes, mainline churches *do* believe in getting saved." But that begs the question "What does it *mean* to be saved?"

Where I live in the Bible-belt South, we usually think of getting saved in the following way: A person goes to an evangelistic worship service, perhaps a revival meeting. After some spirited singing, the preacher preaches a passionate sermon about the need to get saved. After the sermon comes the invitation. The congregation begins to sing "Just as I Am," and people are encouraged to walk down the aisle and accept Jesus. Many verses are sung while the preacher pleads with people to come to Jesus. Finally a person walks down the aisle, usually with tears in their eyes, and prays with the preacher to accept Jesus as "Savior and Lord." And that's how someone is saved.

Two questions come to mind when I think about that scenario: (1) Do *some* people get saved this way? The answer is—absolutely. That is a perfectly valid way to become a Christian. (2) Do *all* people get saved this way? The answer is—absolutely not. Most people do *not* get saved this way. In fact, that kind of emotional altar call at an evangelistic service is relatively new to Christianity. Evangelistic altar calls did not even exist until the early 1800s in the American West. Most denominations today *never* have evangelistic altar-call invitations. In fact, highly emotional, sometimes manipulative altar calls usually turn people off, much like a pushy car salesperson. People rarely make life-changing spiritual decisions on the spot. They need time to think about, pray through, and process their decision. So, while *some* people get saved during an altar-call invitation, the vast majority of Christians, past and present, have *never* had that kind of experience. Getting saved is not about walking down an aisle at church. Which brings me back to the question: What does it mean to be saved? To help answer that question, I first need to lay out three foundational affirmations concerning salvation.

Three Affirmations Concerning Salvation

1. *Salvation is a lifelong process.* Getting saved is not a one-time experience. Instead, salvation is a lifelong journey of relating to God. For example, when Jesus called people to himself, he did not say, "Here are four spiritual laws you must believe," or "Here's a sinner's prayer you must say." No, Jesus simply said, "Follow me." We see an example of that in Matthew 9:9 when Jesus invites Matthew to follow him. Matthew does so, and in the months and years

that followed, he experiences salvation. The apostle Paul understood that salvation was a lifelong process. In Philippians 2, Paul says, "Continue to work out your salvation with fear and trembling" (v. 12 NIV). Salvation is not a one-shot deal but a lifelong process and journey.

2. *We are saved by God's grace.* Salvation comes from God and only from God. As Ephesians 2:8 says, "For it is by grace you have been saved, through faith—and this not from yourselves, it is the gift of God—not by works, so that no one can boast" (NIV). We don't earn salvation. We don't deserve it. Salvation is pure gift and pure grace.

3. *Salvation requires human response.* Although salvation is a gift from God, we have to *accept* that gift. For example, in the book of Acts, a jailer asks Paul and Silas, "What must I do to be saved?" Paul and Silas reply, "Believe in the Lord Jesus, and you will be saved" (Acts 16:30–31). Before salvation is fully experienced, there must be a human response of faith. However, even our ability to respond to God is a gift of God's grace. So in the end, salvation is all about the grace of God.

With that as background, I will lay out the official United Methodist doctrine of salvation, which is similar to all mainline churches. Although our doctrine of salvation comes from John Wesley, the founder of the Methodist Church, Wesley took it from the Bible. Let's call it "The Three Steps of Salvation."

The Three Steps of Salvation

Step 1: God's prevenient grace. Prevenient grace is grace that *draws us toward God.* I know "prevenient" is a strange word. It comes from John Wesley's era, which was a different age from ours, and they used a different vocabulary. A more modern term would be God's *preceding* grace—grace that precedes, or goes before, conscious faith. Another way of putting it is God's *preparing* grace.

God's prevenient grace is God's act of wooing us to God. Even before we are aware of God, God is at work, drawing us to faith. We see that throughout the Bible. For example, Jeremiah 31 says, "I have loved you with an everlasting love; I have *drawn* you with loving-kindness" (v. 3 NIV, with added emphasis). In Ezekiel we read, "For this is what the Sovereign Lord says: I myself will *search* for my sheep. . . . I will search for the lost and *bring back* the strays" (34:11, 16 NIV, with added emphasis). In the Gospel of John, Jesus says, "No one can come to me unless the Father who sent me *draws* him" (6:44 NIV, with added emphasis).

God uses many different means to draw people to faith. For example, when a nonbeliever looks out at a sunset and thinks that surely there must be a Creator, that's prevenient grace in action. God can use a crisis in a person's life to make someone more spiritually receptive. God does not *cause* the crisis but can *use* it to draw people to faith. For example, the death of a loved one, a divorce, or a job layoff often makes people realize they need strength beyond themselves. Other people are drawn to God because of internal emptiness. They begin to think, *There has to be more to life than just making a living.* When they think those thoughts, God is at work, drawing them toward salvation.

Although prevenient grace can be found anywhere, it's especially at work in the life of the church. For example, when we baptize infants, God's prevenient grace is powerfully at work. Even before that child understands anything about God, God is drawing that child to God's self. Children will one day need to affirm faith for themselves, usually at confirmation. But from the beginning, God is calling children into a relationship with God's self. Sometimes God uses Holy Communion to help draw people to faith, making them more receptive to spiritual concerns.

God often uses worship services, small-group classes, and other church activities to help launch people on a journey toward God and toward salvation. This is what we mean by prevenient grace. It's the grace of God that woos us and draws us toward God.

Step 2: God's justifying grace. Justifying grace is *grace that makes us right with God.* When people speak about getting "saved," this is usually what they are referring to. Justifying grace happens when a person intentionally and consciously accepts God's love, pardon, and forgiveness by affirming faith in Jesus Christ. We read about this kind of grace in the book of Romans. In 5:1, for example, Paul says, "Therefore, since we are justified by faith, we have peace with God through our Lord Jesus Christ." In other words, we are made right with God through faith in the life, death, and resurrection of Jesus Christ. When we affirm faith in Christ we are justified by God, made right with God, and are saved. At that point, if we have not already been baptized, we will want to be baptized. And, if we are not already church members, we will want to become members of God's church.

It is important to note that justification can happen in two different ways. Justification can happen *suddenly*, or it can happen *gradually*. Both are valid. For me, justifying grace happened suddenly. I was not brought up in church. The first time I ever attended church, I was fifteen years old. However, before I attended that worship service, God's prevenient grace had already been at work in my life, drawing me to Christ. When I walked into church that day, God's preparing grace had already made me ripe for faith. So when I heard the simple message of salvation that day, I affirmed faith in Jesus. I walked down the aisle of a Baptist church, prayed to receive Jesus, and was saved. It happened suddenly.

However, other people have different experiences. Take for example, the associate pastor at my church. He had a completely different salvation experience. He was raised in the church from the day he was born. Actually, he came to church *before* he was born, in his mother's womb. He has always been surrounded by Christian faith. Therefore he never had a sudden experience of justifying grace. Instead, he has always been in the loving arms of Jesus. Certainly a time came in his life when he recognized and affirmed that he was a person of faith; but it came *gradually*, through the years in his faith community. That's the experience of most mainline Christians. And that kind of gradual faith is just as valid as sudden faith. In fact, for people brought up in the life of the church, gradual faith is the norm.

This kind of gradual faith is often publicly expressed at confirmation. At confirmation, a young person says, "My faith is not just my parent's faith anymore, or just my church's faith, but *my* faith." That kind of gradual faith is the way most people come to Christ, including Ruth Graham, Billy Graham's wife, now deceased. Almost everyone has heard of the famous evangelist Billy Graham. Billy Graham can tell you the exact day when he experienced God's justifying grace and became a Christian. It happened to him suddenly. But Billy Graham's wife, Ruth, had a different experience. She once said, "I have never known a time when I was not a Christian." Justifying grace came to Ruth Graham gradually, over time. Both ways of experiencing God's justifying grace, sudden or gradual, are perfectly valid. In both cases people affirm their faith in the life, death, and resurrection of Jesus Christ, and they are saved.

Step 3: God's sanctifying grace. Sanctifying grace is *grace that leads us toward spiritual maturity.* When we accept God's justifying grace and find pardon and forgiveness, that's just the *beginning* of salvation, the initial step. From that point onward, God wants us to grow in Christian maturity. We see that throughout the Bible. Leviticus 11:44 says, "I am the Lord your God; consecrate yourselves and be holy, because I am holy" (NIV). Matthew 5:48 says, "Be perfect, therefore, as your heavenly Father is perfect." This is what John Wesley meant when he spoke of "going on toward perfection." Although we won't ever be completely perfect in this life, that's our goal. For example, the book of Hebrews urges us to "go on to maturity" (6:1 NIV). Affirming faith in Jesus is only the beginning of salvation. After that, God wants us to mature and grow deeper in faith and in service. Sanctifying grace is a lifetime journey and concludes only with death, when we meet God in heaven and are finally made perfect, complete, and mature.

Nailing Down Your Salvation

If you are not sure of your salvation, I want to give you an opportunity to nail it down. If you have any doubt that you are saved, you can erase that doubt. The fact that you are reading this book and thinking about faith tells me that you've already experienced God's prevenient grace. Clearly, God is calling you to faith.

Therefore, the next step is to accept God's justifying grace. If you have never affirmed faith in Jesus Christ, or if you are not sure that you have, you can do so right now by praying the following prayer. You don't have to say these exact words: you can use your own words, but use this prayer as a guide:

> Dear God, thank you for loving me and offering me salvation. I joyfully accept your forgiveness and grace. The best I know how, I affirm faith in the life, death, and resurrection of Jesus Christ, and I accept him as my Savior. Thank you for adopting me as your child. Help me faithfully to follow you for the rest of my life. I pray in Jesus' name. Amen.

If you pray that prayer, or if you have prayed it some-time in the past—and you mean it—you are saved. Nail that down in your heart and in your mind. *You are saved!* If you have never been baptized before, you will want to do so. And if you are not yet an active member of a church, you need to become one. Any pastor of any denomination will be happy to talk with you about baptism and church membership.

After experiencing God's prevenient grace and accept-ing God's justifying grace, it's time to move on toward God's sanctifying grace. This involves practicing spiritual disciplines such as prayer, Bible study, congregational worship, financial stewardship, service to others, and join-ing a small group of believers like a Sunday school class for spiritual growth and Christian friendship. Your pastor and church can help you on this important journey of "moving on toward perfection."

❊ ❊ ❊

Bottom line: *So do mainline Christians believe in getting saved? You bet we do!*

CONCLUSION

⸻ ∽∾ ⸻

We've covered a lot of territory in this little book. But in the end there are only three points. First, Christians *don't* need to believe in closed-minded faith. Second, Christians *do* need to believe in Jesus. And third, our beliefs in Jesus answer many of life's most important questions.

In conclusion, I'd like to make three final comments. First, this book was never intended to be a comprehensive overview of Christian theology. There is much we did not cover, and what we did cover was only the basic ABCs of Christian belief. Second, Christian faith is far *more* than a set of beliefs. At heart, Christianity is a way of life. What we *do* is more important than what we believe. Third, it's impossible to live out the Christian faith alone. Every believer needs to be part of a local church family. So as strongly as I know how, I encourage you to find a church and root yourself in it. My suggestion is that you find a vibrant mainline church in a United Methodist, Lutheran, Episcopal, Presbyterian, Disciples of Christ, United Church of Christ, or American Baptist denomination. Although this is not an exhaustive list, it's a good starting point. Another option is to connect with a moderate evangelical church like the ones associated with the Cooperative Baptist Fellowship or the Alliance of Baptists.

I have thoroughly enjoyed sharing my thoughts on faith with you. I hope that what I have written has proved helpful to you. If so, please pass the book along to a friend. Better yet, have your entire church study the book together. For more information on how to do so, see the following page.

STUDY GUIDE

INTRODUCTION
TO THE STUDY GUIDE

Mainline and moderate Christians have a compelling faith story to tell. And Americans, more than ever, are eager to hear that story. In postreligious-right America, people are hungry for vibrant, grace-filled, open-minded, centrist, mainline faith. *What's the Least I Can Believe and Still Be a Christian?* can help your church proclaim the good news of mainline and moderate faith to your community.

What Is It?

What's the Least I Can Believe and Still Be a Christian? is a seven-week, easily implemented, worship and Sunday school-based, congregation-wide initiative for mainline and moderate churches.

How Can It Help Your Church?

This unique local-church initiative can help energize your congregation, reach new people, make your church more visible in your community, attractively communicate moderate and mainline faith, wake up your Sunday school classes, and help prepare seven weeks of sermons and worship services without impacting your church budget.

How Does It Work?

The program has three basic components. First, participating churches will encourage their congregation to read an engaging new book about mainline faith called *What's the Least I Can Believe and Still Be a Christian?* Since individual members and not the church will purchase the books, it will not impact the church budget. Second, church leaders will plan seven compelling sermons, worship services, and Sunday school lessons around the content of the book. Sermon helps and small-group lesson plans are provided in this Study Guide. Third, church members will use the book and seven-week event to invite and welcome people to their church. Comprehensive promotional helps for inviting and welcoming people are also included in this Study Guide.

Author Information

Martin Thielen currently serves as senior pastor of Brentwood United Methodist Church, Brentwood, Tennessee, one of the largest United Methodist Churches in America. Before moving to Brentwood, Martin served as senior pastor of First United Methodist Church, Lebanon, Tennessee. During his tenure the church has experienced significant revitalization and growth. Martin has a bachelor of arts, a master of divinity, and a doctor of ministry degrees, along with a year of PhD coursework at Vanderbilt University. He served for four years as a national worship and preaching editor and consultant for the SBC. He has led more than one hundred church leadership workshops for ministers across the country. He also served as an adjunct professor of worship and preaching at a seminary. Writing for publication has long been an important part of Martin's ministry. He has written five books, four of them on the subject of worship and preaching, and more than one hundred articles. His doctor of ministry project was "Ministering to Ministers through Writing." Martin's preaching and worship Web site can be found at www.GettingReadyFor Sunday.com.

LEADING THE
SEVEN-WEEK INITIATIVE

CRYCRY

The following steps will help you carry out the seven-week, congregation-wide initiative at your church.

1. Block out seven consecutive Sunday mornings on the calendar to carry out the event. Scheduling options include Lent, summer, fall, or New Year's. You can also schedule the study for Wednesday or Sunday nights. Even if your congregation does not engage in a churchwide study of the book, individual Sunday school classes or other small groups might want to use it as a resource.

2. Prepare your Sunday school teachers or other small-group leaders for the event. Two to three months before the seven-week initiative, gather your teachers to talk about this special study. Give them a copy of the book's preface and contents, along with the teaching helps for small-group leaders (see pp. 176–91). Encourage each adult class to participate. However, do not force the study on anyone. If a particular class doesn't want to participate, that's OK. Most if not all of your adult classes will be excited and enthusiastic about the study.

3. Consider creating a new, short-term class specifically for this event. Recruit a few core people to form the class. Ask them to invite members of the congregation who don't normally attend Sunday school to participate during the seven-week study. They can also invite prospective church members to attend the class. A pastor who is not already teaching a class might want to teach this one. After the seven weeks are over, encourage participants of this short-term class to continue meeting for an additional seven weeks, studying unused portions of the book. After that, see if enough interest exists to make the class permanent.

4. Purchase an adequate number of copies of *What's the Least I Can Believe and Still Be a Christian?* Churches who buy multiple copies will receive a discount from the publisher. Any unused books can be returned without penalty. However, laypersons of your congregation, not the church itself, will pay for the books. Encourage all adult members of your congregation, especially members of Sunday school classes or other small groups, to purchase a copy for themselves and additional copies to give to family, friends, neighbors, and coworkers. You can set up a table for purchasing books in the narthex or other heavily trafficked area in your facility. Most members will purchase the books gladly and eagerly. Why? Because church members want to support their church, they want to reach new people for their congregation, and they want to learn more about their faith. This seven-week event will help them do all three. If you prefer, you can purchase the books out of your education and/or evangelism budget. For more information about ordering books, go here: www.thethoughtful christian.com.

5. Begin promoting the seven-week event. In the next section of this Study Guide, you will find several no-cost

or low-cost promotional aids—including a pastoral letter to the congregation, a newsletter article, church bulletin announcements, e-mail promotions, bulletin inserts, newspaper ads or articles, and posters—that church members can send to their friends. One of the major goals of the initiative is for the church to invite and welcome guests. Therefore, encourage your congregation to give copies of the book to family members, friends, coworkers, and neighbors, along with an invitation to attend worship and Sunday school during the seven-week initiative. As you get closer to the start date, ask members to begin reading the book. At the same time, encourage them to give copies of the book to their friends and invite them to worship and Sunday school for the seven-week initiative.

6. Carry out the seven-week series. During the series you will see increased attendance in worship and Sunday school (or other small groups engaged in the study). Current members will be enriched by the inspiring worship services and thought-provoking small-group studies, and new people will be attracted to your church. Carefully follow up with all visitors, both during and after the event.

PROMOTING THE
SEVEN-WEEK INITIATIVE

Pastoral Letter

Six weeks before the event begins, send this letter to all members and friends of the congregation. For best results, send it on church stationery and mail it first-class.

[Date]

[Name]
[Address]

Dear Church Family [if possible, replace "Church Family" with actual names]:

On Sunday, [date], our congregation will embark on an exciting seven-week journey. Our entire church family, both in Sunday school classes and in worship services, will read and discuss an engaging new book about mainline and moderate Christianity titled *What's the Least I Can Believe and Still Be a Christian?*

During this unique study, we'll discuss several things Christians *don't* need to believe. For example, we don't need to believe that good Christians don't doubt or that it's OK for Christians to be judgmental and obnoxious. However, we'll spend most of our time studying what Christians *do* need to believe. In short, Christians need to believe in Jesus—his life, teachings, example, death, and resurrection. A great benefit of these beliefs is that they provide promising answers to life's most profound questions, including: What matters most? Am I accepted? Where is God? What brings fulfillment? What about suffering? And is there hope?

You can help us prepare for this dynamic seven-week experience in the following ways. First, pray for this important event. Second, attend Sunday school and worship every Sunday during the seven-week initiative. Third, purchase copies of *What's the Least I Can Believe and Still Be a Christian?* for yourself, your family, and your friends. Books can be purchased in the narthex on Sunday mornings or in the church office during the week. Finally, invite family members, friends, neighbors, and coworkers to visit our church during the seven-week event.

I look forward to this special time together. Please contact me if you have any questions. It's a joy to be your pastor!

In Christ's love and service,

[your name]

Newsletter Article

As soon as the pastoral letter goes out, place the same letter (minus the greeting and conclusion) in the newsletter—as seen below. Continue to put this in the newsletter until the event has begun. Repetition is good when you are trying to communicate with an entire congregation. You cannot overcommunicate!

What's the Least I Can Believe and Still Be a Christian?

On Sunday, [date], our congregation will embark on an exciting seven-week journey. Our entire church family, both in Sunday school classes and in worship services, will read and discuss an engaging new book about mainline and moderate Christianity titled *What's the Least I Can Believe and Still Be a Christian?*

During this unique study we'll discuss several things Christians *don't* need to believe. For example, we don't need to believe that good Christians don't doubt or that it's OK for Christians to be judgmental and obnoxious. However, we'll spend most of our time studying what Christians *do* need to believe. In short, Christians need to believe in Jesus—his life, teachings, example, death, and resurrection. A great benefit of these beliefs is that they provide promising answers to life's most profound questions, including: What matters most? Am I accepted? Where is God? What brings fulfillment? What about suffering? And is there hope?

You can help us prepare for this dynamic seven-week experience in the following ways. First, pray for this important event. Second, attend Sunday school and worship every Sunday during the seven-week initiative. Third, purchase copies of *What's the Least I Can Believe and Still Be a Christian?* for yourself, your family, and your friends. Books can be purchased in the narthex on Sunday mornings or in the church office during the week. Finally, invite family members, friends, neighbors, and coworkers to visit our church during the seven-week event.

Church Bulletin Announcements

Six weeks in advance of the event, begin placing the following announcement in the church bulletin. Continue to run this announcement until the event begins:

On Sunday, [date], our church will embark on an exciting seven-week journey. Our worship services and adult Sunday school classes will focus on an engaging new book about mainline and moderate Christianity titled *What's the Least I Can Believe and Still Be a Christian?* Copies of the book will be available for purchase in the narthex soon. This will be a great time to invite guests to visit our church! For more information, please see the church newsletter and Web site.

Worship Announcements

At least one month before the first session/sermon, begin making verbal announcements in the worship services each week about the upcoming seven-week initiative.

Phone Campaign

One month before the event begins, recruit a telephone task force. People on this task force will call every member of the congregation, along with prospective members. They will remind or inform them of the event and invite them to attend. Two weeks before the event begins, have the task force begin making the calls. Complete the calls at least five days before the first Sunday of the initiative.

Posters

Four weeks in advance of the event, create posters and place them throughout your church and around the community.

E-mail Promotion

Two weeks in advance of the event, send the following e-mail to your congregation. Ask them to forward it to all their family members and friends, along with an invitation to visit our church during the seven-week event. One week in advance of the event, send this same e-mail again:

What's the Least I Can Believe
and Still Be a Christian?

A Seven-Week Series
for Mainline and Moderate Christians

Week 1: (Don't) Gimme Me That Old-Time Religion
Week 2: Jesus' Priority: What Matters Most?
Week 3: Jesus' Grace: Am I Accepted?
Week 4: Jesus' Work: Where Is God?
Week 5: Jesus' Example: What Brings Fulfillment?
Week 6: Jesus' Death: What about Suffering?
Week 7: Jesus Resurrection: Is There Hope?

Include the name of your church, the dates of the event, worship times, Sunday school times, church address, Web site address, and phone number.

Bulletin Inserts

Use the same information and layout as the above e-mail flyer to make bulletin inserts. Place them in the church bulletin the two Sundays before the event begins. Encourage people to give or mail them to family, friends, neighbors, and coworkers, along with an invitation to attend church during the seven-week event. Place additional copies of the inserts in the narthex. Right before the benediction, remind the congregation about the additional inserts available in the narthex. Encourage them to take extra copies to give or mail to family and friends.

Newspaper Ads

If you have an advertising or evangelism budget, place the above bulletin insert or e-mail flyer in newspaper ads beginning two weeks before the event.

Newspaper Article

Many local newspapers are willing to run church stories, especially if the articles are ready for publication. Two weeks before the event, submit the following article to your local newspaper. Tell them you would greatly appreciate their running the story. The best time for the story to run is the Monday or Tuesday before the event begins on Sunday. A photo of the church and/or a photo of the front cover of the book would be a nice addition to the story.

Unique Event
at [name of your church]

Beginning on Sunday, [date], [name of church] will begin a unique seven-week event called *What's the Least I Can Believe and Still Be a Christian?* This congregation and community-wide event will be based on an engaging new book about mainline and moderate Christianity. Participants will study things Christians *don't* need to believe, as well as things Christians *do* need to believe. The entire community is invited to attend. The series will continue every Sunday morning through [closing date]. Sunday worship services are held at [time of service/s]. Sunday school classes are held at [time of classes]. [name of church] is located at [address]. For further information, see its Web site at [Web address] or call the church office at [phone number].

TIME LINE
FOR PROMOTION

Two months in advance of the event:

- Block out seven consecutive Sundays to carry out the initiative.
- Meet with your Sunday school and/or small-group leaders to explain the event and get them on board.
- Order books (bulk discounts are available).

Six weeks in advance of the event:

- Mail the pastor's letter.
- Publish article in newsletter and repeat it until the event begins.
- Place announcement in bulletin and repeat it until the event begins.
- Find a core group of people to form and promote the short-term class.
- Place information about the event on your Web site and leave it up until the event is completed.

Four weeks in advance of the event:

- Begin selling books in narthex and church office.

- Place posters around the church and community.
- Begin making verbal announcements in worship.
- Recruit telephone task force.

Three weeks in advance of the event:

- Begin inviting people to the new short-term class.

Two weeks in advance of the event:

- Send e-mail promotion to congregation.
- Place inserts in bulletins with additional copies in narthex.
- Place ads in local newspaper(s).
- Send article to local newspaper(s).
- Begin telephone campaign.

One week in advance of the event:

- Send another e-mail promotion.
- Complete the telephone campaign.

CUSTOMIZING THE
SEVEN-WEEK INITIATIVE

∞

Since *What's the Least I Can Believe and Still Be a Christian?* has twenty-one chapters, churches will not be able to cover the entire book during the seven-week initiative. After the seven-week event is over, many classes will want to return to the book and study the remaining chapters that interest them. This will provide small groups with up to fourteen additional weeks of study at no additional cost.

We suggest the following schedule for the seven-week emphasis. However, as you will see below, you can customize the study to fit your church's interests and needs. Comprehensive sermon helps and small-group study guides for all seven weeks can be found later in this guide.

Suggested Seven-Week Schedule

Week 1: Introduction to *What's the Least I Can Believe and Still Be a Christian?* The first Sunday will introduce the congregation-wide initiative by broaching a few ideas from part 1 of the book. However, we do not expect pastors to preach on the more controversial subjects during the seven-week series. That's best left to small groups after the series is over. After noting a few things that Christians *don't* need to believe, the question will be raised: What *do* Christians need to believe? The answer, of course, is Jesus.

Week 2: Jesus' Priority: What Matters Most? (chap. 12 in the book)

Week 3: Jesus' Grace: Am I Accepted? (chap. 13)

Week 4: Jesus' Work: Where Is God? (chap. 14)

Week 5: Jesus' Example: What Brings Fulfillment? (chap. 15)

Week 6: Jesus' Death: What about Suffering? (chap. 16)

Week 7: Jesus Resurrection: Is There Hope? (chap. 17)

This selection of chapters will resonate with your members and attract guests. If you like, however, you can substitute chapters. For example, you could drop chapter 15, "Jesus' Example: What Brings Fulfillment?" and substitute chapter 20, "Jesus' Vision: What Is God's Dream for the World?" You can also extend the series beyond seven weeks, perhaps going eight or nine weeks. For example, on the second Sunday of the initiative, you could add chapter 11, "Jesus' Identity: Who Is Jesus?" and thus extend the event to eight Sundays. Or you can delete one or two of the suggested chapters and reduce the event to five or six weeks. In short, each church can customize the event to meet its own unique needs.

TEACHING HELPS
FOR SMALL-GROUP LEADERS

ᗯᗢᗯ

Thank you for leading a small group for *What's the Least I Can Believe and Still Be a Christian?* The small-group component is a crucial part of this event, so you are playing an important role in the life of your church.

Suggestions for leading each of the seven weeks follow. Each lesson plan includes a bottom-line summary of the lesson, Scripture references, a brief commentary of the text/s, a video recommendation, discussion questions, and a closing prayer. Feel free to add to, subtract from, or adapt these ideas to meet the needs of your unique class.

A Note about Using Video

Be mindful of the warning at the beginning of videotapes or DVDs that you rent or purchase. The rental or purchase of such videos gives you the right to show them in a home setting only, unless you purchase a license to show them elsewhere. Check with your pastor or director of education to see if your church or school already has such a license.

Week 1: (Don't) Gimme
That Old-Time Religion

Bottom Line of Lesson

Some old-time religion is unhealthy and needs to be discarded.

Scripture Texts

Matthew 9:16–17
Matthew 19:3–9
Matthew 23:13–15, 25–28

Brief Commentary on the Texts

Matthew 9:16–17: Jesus speaks of old wineskins, a reference to the old-time religion of his day. Jesus said that sometimes new wineskins are needed because some old-time religion isn't worth keeping.

Matthew 19:3–9: In Jesus' day old-time religion allowed a man to divorce his wife for any reason. In a day without alimony, child support, or public assistance of any kind, it usually left her with two options: begging or prostitution. That was old-time religion, and Jesus completely rejected it.

Matthew 23:13–15, 25–28: Jesus chastises some of the religious leaders of his day for their toxic faith, especially their arrogance, pride, and hypocrisy.

Sunday Morning at the Movies

To help introduce the theme, consider showing the final two to three minutes of the movie *Religulous*. This film argues that all religion is toxic and needs to be discarded. It could spark spirited dialogue about the subject of unhealthy religion.

Discussion Starters

1. In the preface of the book, the author tells a story about a young man named Danny:

> When I first met Danny, he said, "Preacher, you need to know that I'm an atheist. I don't believe the Bible. I don't like organized religion. And I can't stand self-righteous, judgmental Christians."
>
> In spite of Danny's avowed atheism and my devout Christian beliefs, we became close friends. Over the next year Danny and I engaged in numerous conversations about God, religion, and faith. During that time Danny softened his stance on atheism. One day, after a long conversation, he announced with a laugh, "I've decided to upgrade from an atheist to an agnostic." Several months later Danny said, "I've had an epiphany. I realize that I don't reject Christianity. Instead, I reject the way that intolerant Christians *package* Christianity."

Can you relate to Danny's comments? What "packages" of Christianity turn you off? Why?

2. What examples of unhealthy religion do you see in the world today?

3. Read Matthew 23:13–15, 25–28. In this passage, Jesus condemns the toxic faith of some of the religious leaders of his day. How does this text make you feel? Does it trouble you to hear Jesus speak such harsh words? Why was Jesus so unhappy with these people? (If time permits, read and discuss the other two texts listed above.)

4. In recent years several popular books have been arguing that all religion is toxic and therefore needs to

be rejected. Examples include *The God Delusion* and *God Is Not Great*. The film *Religulous* makes the same argument. (This would be a good time to show the movie clip mentioned above.) How do you respond to the argument that all religion is unhealthy and needs to be abandoned?

5. In the introduction to part 1, the author says:

A lot of old-time religion is good and noble, and we'll explore much of it in part 2 of this book. But some old-time religion is neither good nor noble. Old-time religion gave us the Crusades, the Inquisition, and religious wars. Old-time religion oppressed woman, defended slavery, and stifled scientific inquiry. The fact is, some of that old-time religion is unhealthy and needs to be discarded. In the chapters that follow, we will review ten tenets of old-time religion that Christians can and should discard.

The author then reviews ten tenets of old-time faith that he thinks we should discard. We don't have time to review all those today or even in this seven-week study, but we can return to them later. Let's quickly review those ten chapter titles. (Have the class look at the contents, part 1.) Which of these chapter titles do you tend to agree with? Which ones make you uncomfortable? Why? Which ones would you like to study after the seven-week initiative is over?

Who's Not Here?
Before you conclude today's class, talk about people who could be invited to the class, both church members and potential members. Get volunteers from your class to call and invite each person named to the remainder of the seven-week study.

Closing Prayer

Dear God, we are all capable of having unhealthy religion. Forgive us when we let our religion become unhealthy. Help us instead to have vibrant, healthy, life-giving faith. Empower us to live out that kind of faith and to share it with others. We pray in Christ's name. Amen.

Week 2: Jesus' Priority: What Matters Most?

Bottom Line of Lesson

Relationships — with God and others — matter most.

Scripture Text

Mark 12:28–34

Brief Commentary on the Text

Jesus lays out the most important element of life and faith: loving God and loving others.

Sunday Morning at the Movies

For fun, and to help introduce the theme, show a brief movie clip from *Up in the Air*. The clip can be found in chapter 13 of the DVD (81:36 to 82:36). In this clip a young man, terrified of getting married, starting a family, and growing old, asks the question "What's the point?"

Discussion Starters

1. What do Americans value most? List answers on the board. Examples would include money, career, success, beauty, fame, status, family, faith, country, and so forth. Ask the class to decide which three of these items are most

important to most Americans. Then ask, How important do you think these three things are to Jesus?

2. Ask members of the class each to make their own "top three" list. Ask them to share what they are and why they picked those particular items. Ask them if their "top three" have changed over the years, and if so, why?

3. Read today's text. Ask, What does it mean to love God with all our heart, mind, soul, and strength? What does it mean to love our neighbor as ourselves?

4. Have someone in the class read the opening story about Steve and Lisa. After the reading, ask participants to respond to the story. What feelings did it evoke? What thoughts?

5. Ask, If our relationship with God and others truly is the most important thing in our lives, how would that impact the way we live? What would we do differently?

Closing Prayer

Help us Lord, to love you with all our heart, mind, soul, and strength, and help us to love our neighbors as ourselves. Amen.

Week 3: Jesus' Grace: Am I Accepted?

Bottom Line of Lesson

In his grace, Jesus loves and accepts us, even with our flaws, as beloved children of God.

Scripture Texts

Matthew 9:10–13
John 8:1–11

Brief Commentary on the Texts

Matthew 9:10–13: The religious authorities are upset when Jesus eats dinner with a group of sinners, but Jesus reminds them that God is a God of mercy and that Jesus has come to call not the righteous but sinners.

John 8:1–11: Ancient Jewish law called for execution of adulterers. However, when a woman was caught in adultery Jesus offered her grace. His statement "Let anyone among you who is without sin be the first to throw a stone at her" is one of the most famous quotes of the Bible.

Sunday Morning at the Movies

Watch a video clip depicting the story of the woman caught in adultery from the old movie *Jesus of Nazareth*. It might be available at a local video rental store. You can also get the clip at www.wingclips.com. Look under the topic "judging," and then find *Jesus of Nazareth*. Perhaps a technologically gifted member of the class could burn it onto a DVD and bring it for viewing, if you have the legal license to do so. Or perhaps the class could watch it on a laptop computer. The clip is called "First Stone." It lasts just under three minutes.

Discussion Starters

1. What if everyone received exactly what they deserved? Would that be a good thing, or not?

2. What does the word "grace" mean to you?

3. Think of a time when you received grace. What did it feel like? How did it impact you?

4. Have someone read the first four paragraphs of the chapter. Ask the class to respond to the argument that grace is the one belief unique to Christianity.

5. Read John 8:1–11. Watch the video if it's available. What feelings does this story evoke in you? How do you think this woman felt? Why was the man not accused of anything?

6. Ask someone in the class to read the final story of the chapter: "Dancing with Grace." Ask class members if they are comfortable with this image of God? If so, why? If not, why not?

Closing Prayer
Eternal God, thank you for your unmerited, unconditional, amazing grace. Help us to freely receive that grace in our lives, and help us to freely give it to others. In Christ's name. Amen.

Week 4: Jesus' Work: Where Is God?

Bottom Line of Lesson
Although God is not limited to working through people, God primarily works in the world incarnationally — through human instruments.

Scripture Text
John 1:1–5, 14

Brief Commentary on the Text
Jesus has coexisted with God (and the Holy Spirit) from the beginning of time. However, at the appointed hour, God sent Jesus to earth. Thus God became "flesh."

We call this the "incarnation." In short, the incarnation tells us that God actively engages in the world through human beings, especially through Jesus Christ.

Sunday Morning at the Movies

In the introduction of the chapter, the author uses two films to illustrate two competing theories about how God works in the world. Show a brief clip from both movies. For *The Truman Show*, see chapter 20, minutes 83:18–84:47. For *Apollo 13*, see chapter 12, minutes 79:57–81:02.

Discussion Starters

1. Ask the class to give biblical examples of God's using human beings to do God's work. For example, Adam and Eve tended the garden and named the animals, Noah built an ark, Abraham and Sarah began a nation, David led the people of Israel, and so on.

2. Ask the class to give modern examples of God's using human beings to do God's work. For example, pastors preaching the gospel, doctors healing the sick, teachers teaching children, parents raising responsible children, and so forth.

3. Ask, Where is God at work in our congregation and community? How can we cooperate with God to do God's work in this place?

4. Watch the two video clips mentioned above. Discuss the two different versions of how God works in the world. See the opening paragraphs of the chapter for guidance in this discussion.

5. On the Internet find the lyrics for "Who Will Be Jesus?" by Bruce Carroll. (Copyright laws prevent us

from printing them here.) Have someone read them. Ask for feedback.

Closing Prayer

Thank you, Lord, for working in the world through ordinary people like us. Use each one of us here today to help carry out your work in our church and community. In Christ's name. Amen.

Week 5: Jesus' Example: What Brings Fulfillment?

Bottom Line of Lesson

True fulfillment comes from serving others.

Scripture Text

John 13:1–5, 13–17

Brief Commentary on the Text

Jesus washes his disciples' feet and then uses that experience to teach them about the importance of service. By taking on the role of a servant and washing his disciples' feet, Jesus shows us that true fulfillment comes from caring for others. As Jesus said in today's text, when we follow his example and serve other people, we "will be blessed" (v. 17 NIV).

Sunday Morning at the Movies

Near the end of the chapter, you will find a section called "Dr. Green's Final Prescription." It's based on the television show *ER*. In this scene Dr. Mark Green, a major character in the show, gives his final advice to his daughter before he dies from a brain tumor. His final advice is "Be generous." You can find this episode on Season 8 of *ER*, "On the Beach" (November 13, 2008).

Discussion Starters

1. The opening section of this chapter tells the story of Millard Fuller, founder of Habitat for Humanity. Have any of you ever volunteered on a Habitat build? Tell us about that experience. What did it mean to you to work on the house?

2. What's the most significant service experience you have ever had? What impact did it have on you?

3. In this chapter the author says:

Self-absorbed people who live only for themselves and their immediate family will never be content. Self is too small a god to serve. True fulfillment comes only through service to others. Hundreds of different ways exist for us to follow Jesus' example. But every Christian is called by God to pick up a towel and wash the feet of others in some way. And when we do, we—like Millard Fuller of Habitat for Humanity—will discover true joy and fulfillment.

Respond to that statement. Has that been true in your life?

4. What are some practical ways we can serve others in our church and community? What can our Sunday school class do to serve others?

5. Read the text about Jesus' washing the feet of the disciples. How do you think it would feel to have Jesus wash your feet? What was Jesus trying to teach them?

6. Watch the *ER* clip mentioned above. How did that scene make you feel? If you were going to give your child or children your last advice, what would it be?

Closing Prayer

Thank you, Lord, for the gift of service. Help us to take up our towels and wash others' feet. Help us to better serve our family, our friends, our church, and our community. Through Christ our Lord we pray. Amen.

Week 6: Jesus' Death: What about Suffering?

Bottom Line of Lesson

Although God does not prevent suffering, the crucified God fully enters human suffering and works to redeem that suffering.

Scripture Text

Matthew 27:27–31

Brief Commentary on the Text

A major portion of each Gospel is devoted to Jesus' crucifixion, including this brief passage of Christ's passion. The death of Christ was extremely important to the biblical writers. Jesus' suffering tells us that, at heart, God is a crucified God who fully understands and enters human suffering.

Sunday Morning at the Movies

Show a brief clip from *The Passion of the Christ*. See chapter 16, minutes 53:13–54:53.

Discussion Starters

1. This week's chapter raises two important questions about suffering. First, why does suffering occur? Second, where is God when suffering occurs? Today we'll discuss those two questions. We'll begin with

the question, Why does suffering occur? In this chapter the author lists several answers to that question, including these: (1) human sin, (2) the laws of nature, (3) an opportunity for us to grow, and (4) demonic forces of evil. (List these on the board.) How helpful are these answers to you? Can you think of others? (Note: Since this is such a complex topic, the discussion today will need to be done in a brief, broad-strokes fashion. You can come back later and discuss this more in-depth, including studying chapter 1, "God Causes Cancer, Car Wrecks, and Other Catastrophes.")

2. The second question raised in today's chapter is, Where is God when suffering occurs? The author says:

> When children get leukemia, teenagers die in accidents, good Christian people contract Lou Gehrig's disease, or communities are devastated by tornadoes, where is God? That's a profoundly important question. The Christian answer to that question is clear. There's no ambiguity here, no "seeing through the glass dimly." Instead, the answer is straightforward. Where is God in the midst of suffering? God is right smack in the middle of it. We learn that from the cross of Jesus.

What response do you have to that quote? Does the concept of a "crucified God" who enters human suffering resonate with you? Why? Why not?

3. Have you ever experienced God's presence in suffering? Would you be willing to tell us about that experience?

4. Watch the above video clip from *The Passion of the Christ*. How did you feel as you watched that clip? What does it mean to you that Jesus was tortured and executed?

5. Read the final section of the chapter, "The Cruci-fied God." Ask members of the class to respond to that story.

Closing Prayer
Lord, we acknowledge today that we don't have final answers to the problem of suffering. But we thank you for being a God who understands, enters, and ultimately redeems suffering. Today we pray for those who suf-fer, including members of our class and church. Through Christ our Lord. Amen.

Week 7: Jesus' Resurrection: Is There Hope?

Bottom Line of Lesson
Jesus Christ's resurrection gives us hope for life and even hope for death.

Scripture Text
Matthew 28:1–7

Brief Commentary on the Text
This passage, along with other Gospel narratives of the resurrection, proclaim the glorious good news: "He is not here; for he has been raised!"

Sunday Morning at the Movies
The end of the chapter has a section called "The Last Word Is Hope." It's based on the movie *The Shawshank Redemption*. If you would like to use a brief video presen-tation from the movie, use the following clips: (1) 71:27–72:56 and (2) 134:30–136:15, followed immediately by (3) 136:56–138:13. Another option is to watch the

powerful video *Sunday's Coming* (http://www.ignitermedia
.com).

Discussion Starters

1. Hope is a major biblical theme. Why do you think
that is the case?

2. Think of a time when hope helped you through a
rough experience. Would you be willing to share that with
the group?

3. How important is the resurrection of Christ to
Christianity? Would there be a Christian faith and
church without the resurrection? If so, what would it
look like?

4. In today's text some women went to the tomb where
Jesus was buried and heard the news of Easter: "He is
not here; for he has been raised!" What do you think that
would have been like?

5. When the women first told the other disciples about
the resurrection, they were met with skepticism. Why do
you think that was the case? Do you think it is difficult for
people to believe in the resurrection today?

6. What does the resurrection of Christ mean to you
personally?

7. The last section of the chapter is called "The Last
Word Is Hope." It's based on the movie *The Shawshank
Redemption*. Watch the clips and discuss the theme of hope
in the movie. If you can't watch the clips, have someone
read this portion of the chapter and discuss it.

Closing Prayer

Thank you, Lord, for the great gift of hope, both in this life and in the life to come. Thank you that the last word of the gospel is not death but life, not crucifixion but resurrection, not despair but hope. We give you thanks in the name of the risen Christ. Amen.

PREACHING HELPS
FROM THE AUTHOR

I'm delighted that you and your church are participating in this event! In this section of the Study Guide are preaching materials to help you prepare sermons for the seven-week initiative. Before the preaching suggestions, several comments are in order.

First, one year during the Lenten season, I preached a seven-week sermon series on *What's the Least I Can Believe and Still Be a Christian?* at my church in Lebanon, Tennessee. My congregation and community enthusiastically responded. During the series, worship attendance jumped 20 percent and large numbers of guests visited, and as a direct result of the series, we added over a dozen new members, several by adult affirmation of faith and baptism. If our Sunday school classes had been studying the same seven topics, if we had offered a book on the subject, and if we had promoted it more aggressively, the seven-week event would have been even more effective. If you will carefully prepare and boldly promote it, this seven-week, congregation-wide event can help invigorate your church.

Second, stories from the book will not be duplicated in these preaching helps. But don't be afraid to use content from the book in your sermons, especially the stories. You can feel at ease in using materials from the book for at least three reasons. First, as much as I wish it were so, not everyone at worship during the seven-week event will have read the book! Second, even if they have, they will enjoy hearing the stories again. And third, repetition is a powerful tool, so let it work in your favor.

Preaching ideas for all seven weeks follow.

Week 1: (Don't) Gimme That Old-Time Religion

Matthew 9:16–17; 19:3–9; 23:13–15, 25–28

Introduction to Series

Early in the service, before the Scripture reading and sermon, introduce the series. Tell your congregation how much you are looking forward to the next seven weeks. Encourage those who have not yet read the book to do so. Challenge them to attend one of your small groups during the duration of the series so that they can study the book with others. Explain that in today's service you will be introducing part 1 of the book and that, over the next six weeks, you'll focus on part 2. Print a schedule of the sermon topics in the bulletin, listing which chapter will be covered each Sunday. Call attention to that schedule in this introduction. Finally, remind them that this is a great time to invite guests to church. Conclude this introduction with a prayer, asking God's blessings on the seven-week event.

Unlike sermons 2–7, the first sermon of the series will not come from a specific chapter of the book. Instead, it will be broadly based on part 1 and will serve as an introduction to the entire series. I recommend that you do *not* broach the controversial topics found in part 1 of the book. First, you don't need the grief that comes from preaching on topics like homosexuality! Second, you might not agree with some of my conclusions in part 1. That's OK. Good Christian folks often disagree on difficult issues. Third, these kinds of complex topics are better dealt with in small-group conversational settings than in Sunday morning sermons. Fourth, and perhaps most important, this series is designed, at least in part, to invite and welcome guests to your church. Preaching on highly volatile topics is not a good strategy for welcoming new people. There is certainly a time and place to preach and teach on these topics, but this seven-week initiative is not the best venue. If you want to tackle the hard subjects found in part 1, consider doing a sermon series on those topics at a later date.

The suggested texts for week 1 are Matthew 9:16–17 and Matthew 19:3–9. Both texts provide examples of unhealthy religion. Another good option is Matthew 23:13–15, 25–28, where Jesus takes on the Pharisees for their arrogant, hypocritical, toxic religion. Since the sermon for week 1 does not focus on a specific chapter of the book, I'm providing you with a sermon manuscript. When I preached this introductory sermon at my church, I called it, "(Don't) Give Me That Old-Time Religion."

(Don't) Give Me That Old-Time Religion

Most of you are familiar with the old gospel song "Gimme Me That Old-Time Religion." The chorus goes like this,

"Gimme me that old-time religion, gimme me that old-time religion, gimme me that old-time religion, it's good enough for me." [Note: this will be more effective if you lead them in singing (a cappella) the chorus. If you are not much of a singer, have someone else lead the chorus or ask them to speak the words of the chorus with you.]

Well, a lot of old-time religion is good and noble. But some old-time religion is neither good nor noble. Old-time religion gave us the Crusades, the Inquisition, and religious wars. Old-time religion oppressed woman, defended slavery, and stifled scientific inquiry. The fact is, some old-time religion is unhealthy. Even Jesus didn't like some of that old-time religion. We saw two examples in today's Scripture readings. The first example of Jesus' frustration with old-time religion comes from Matthew 19, which deals with the topic of divorce. In Jesus' day old-time religion allowed a man to divorce his wife for any reason. If she burned his dinner, if he found someone he liked better— the reason didn't matter—he could dump her on the street in a heartbeat. And in a day without alimony, child support, or public assistance of any kind, it usually left her with two options: begging or prostitution. That was old-time religion, and Jesus completely rejected it.

Old-time religion, at least some of it, is greatly overrated. We see the same thing in today's second Scripture reading, from Matthew 9. In this passage Jesus speaks of old wineskins—a clear reference to the old-time religion of his day. Jesus says that sometimes new wineskins are needed because some old-time religion isn't worth keeping. In the book we're studying together, the author mentions ten tenets of old-time religion that can be discarded. Let me quickly review four of them. [Note: you might want to review only one, two, or three of them.]

First, we can discard old-time religion that claims God causes cancer, car wrecks, and other catastrophes. It's not God's will that a nine-year-old child die of leukemia, that a teenager become paralyzed in a car wreck, or that two hundred thousand Haitians die in an earthquake. Just because something bad happens does not mean that God caused it to happen. Jesus understood that. We also need to understand that. Religion that blames God for everything that happens is old-time religion that we can and should discard. [Note: If you want to add further details to any of these four points, add scriptural references, or tell a story to illustrate them, see the corresponding chapters in part 1 of the book. You'll find plenty of material to flesh out these points.]

Second, we can discard old-time religion that claims good Christians don't doubt. Faith is not about having absolute certainty, having all the answers, or seeing everything in black-and-white. Real faith, as the apostle Paul tells us in Corinthians, "sees through the glass dimly." Real faith asks hard questions. Real faith struggles. Real faith doubts. And real faith accepts ambiguity, mystery, and unanswered questions. Even Jesus experienced struggles and questions and doubts. When he was dying on the cross, Jesus cried out, "My God, my God, why have you forsaken me?" Doubt is not the enemy of faith; doubt is a part of faith. So the idea that good Christians don't doubt is old-time religion that we can and should discard.

Third, we can discard old-time religion that claims women can't be preachers and must submit to men. Some Christian leaders, in the name of old-time religion, make women second-class citizens. They insist that women should submit to their husbands, and they insist that women should not serve in leadership roles in the church. They base their argument on a few verses from the Bible. For example, in Ephesians 5, Paul says, "Wives, submit to your husbands." But in the very next chapter, Paul also says, "Slaves, obey your masters." We obviously don't promote slavery anymore, so why would anyone in the twenty-first century promote the submission of women? Mainline Christians understand that women are equal partners with men, that marriage is a partnership and not a hierarchy, and that woman can and should be leaders in the church. So the idea that women are second-class citizens in the home, at church, or in society is old-time religion that we can and should discard.

Finally, we can discard old-time religion that says it's OK for Christians to be judgmental and obnoxious. I'm sure you've met Christians who are arrogant, self-righteous, and judgmental. It's not a new trend. There was a group of people like that in Jesus' time. They were holier than thou, they were judgmental, they believed they had all the right answers, and they condemned everyone who didn't agree with them, including Jesus. They were also the only people whom Jesus didn't like and couldn't get along with. Arrogant, judgmental, obnoxious religion is the exact opposite of the grace-filled spirit of Jesus Christ. It's old-time religion that we can and should discard.

Other examples of unhealthy old-time religion could be mentioned today, but we don't have time for that. So let me get to the bottom line of today's message. Many people in our world today, and in our own community, have problems with religion. However, most of them don't really reject God or Christianity or church. Instead, they reject the way that God and Christianity and church have been *packaged*. In the language of today's text, they are not rejecting the pure wine of Jesus and Christianity; they are rejecting outdated, inadequate, dried-up wineskins. These people desperately need to know about new wineskins. They need to know there are alternative expressions of the Christian faith, different from the negative caricatures they see on religious television and in the news. They need to know that not all Christians reject science and reason. They need to know that not all Christians are judgmental and arrogant. They need to know that it's OK to have questions and doubts. They need to know that you can love God with your heart but also with your head. In short, these people need to know that there are alternatives to unhealthy expressions of old-time religion. And we, as a mainline/moderate church, offer such an alternative. We in the mainline and moderate tradition have a great message of open-minded, grace-filled, gender-equal, "head, heart, and hands," orthodox Christian faith; and we need to proclaim it boldly!

Today we've said that some old-time religion can and should be discarded. But that raises an important question. What old-time religion *cannot* be discarded? That question brings us back to our book. In the preface the author tells an interesting story about a young man named Danny. At first Danny claimed to be an atheist. Later he decided to "upgrade" to an agnostic. Not long after that, Danny was seriously considering becoming a Christian. One day he said to the author of our book, "OK, you've just about convinced me on this religion stuff. So I want to know, what's the least I can believe and still be a Christian?"

"What's the least I can believe and still be a Christian?" What a great question! The answer to that question, of course, is Jesus. We can discard many religious beliefs and still be Christians. However, we cannot discard Jesus. In order to be Christian believers, we must believe in Jesus' life, teaching, example, death, and resurrection. A great benefit of these beliefs is that they provide promising answers to life's most profound questions, including: What matters most? Am I accepted? Where is God? What brings fulfillment? What about suffering? And is there hope? Over the next six weeks we'll explore those questions together. I look forward to the journey!

Week 2: Jesus' Priority:
What Matters Most?

Mark 12:28–34

The text for week 2 is the Great Commandment found in Mark 12. You can get textual help from any good commentary. But to drive the point home, you would do well to tell some stories. You can find several in chapter 12 of the book. For example, consider telling the opening story about Steve and Lisa. This is a powerful story about what matters most in life and would add much to your sermon. You might want to use it as your conclusion. The final story of the chapter, "What about My Résumé?" would also work well. The other stories in chapter 12 come from my own personal experience and might not be as helpful. However, if you take out the personal references made about *Cat on a Hot Tin Roof*, that would also make an excellent illustration. Stories from your own experience would work even better.

Consider beginning the sermon with a scene from the movie *Up in the Air*. If you have projection capabilities, you can show the clip on screen. The one-minute clip comes from chapter 13 (81:36 to 82:36). If you don't use projection screens, just tell the story. In this scene a young man is having second thoughts about getting married. The wedding ceremony is about to begin, but he has a serious case of cold feet. He's not sure he can go through with the wedding. A member of the family, played by George Clooney, is sent to talk to him.

The young man says, "I don't think I'll be able to do this."

George Clooney's character asks, "Why would you say that today?"

The frightened young man says, "Well, last night I was kinda like laying in bed, and I couldn't get to sleep, so

I started thinking about the wedding and the ceremony and about our buying a house, and moving in together, and having a kid, and then having another kid, and then Christmas and Thanksgiving and spring break, and going to football games, and then all of a sudden they are graduated and getting jobs and getting married and, you know, I'm a grandparent, and then I'm retired, and I'm losing my hair, and I'm getting fat, and the next thing I know I'm dead. And it's like, I can't stop from thinking, what's the point? I mean, what is the point?"

That story would be a great jumping-off place to dive into the morning text. When this religious leader asks Jesus, "Of all the commandments, which is the most important?" he was basically asking, "What's the point? What matters most?" There are a lot of answers to that question, from money to success to beauty to power to fame. But Jesus says that what matters most is relationships with God and others. The above movie illustration from *Up in the Air*, along with comments about the text, combined with a strong story or two, will result in an effective sermon for week 2.

The following story would make a good addition to your sermon:

The Big Rocks

A well-known time-management guru gave a speech one day at a top-drawer business school. As he stood in front of a class of high-powered overachievers, he said, "OK, time for a quiz." He pulled out a one-gallon, wide-mouthed Mason jar and set it on the table in front of him. He then produced about a dozen fist-sized rocks and carefully placed them into the jar.

After filling the jar to the top, he asked, "Is this jar full?"

Everyone in the class said, "Yes."

"Really?" he asked. Then he reached under the table and pulled out a bucket of gravel. He poured the gravel into the jar, shaking it as he did, causing pieces of gravel to work themselves into the spaces between the big rocks. Then he asked the group once more, "Is the jar full?"

By now the class was on to him. "Probably not," one of them answered.

"Good answer!" he replied. He reached under the table and brought out a bucket of sand. He dumped the sand into the jar, filling all the spaces between the rocks and the gravel. Once more he asked the question, "Is this jar full?"

"No!" the class shouted.

Once again he said, "Good answer!" Then he took a pitcher of water and poured it until the jar was filled to the brim. He looked at the class and asked, "What is the point of this illustration?"

One eager student said, "No matter how full your schedule, if you try really hard, you can always fit more into it."

"No," the speaker replied, "that's not the point. The point is—if you don't put the big rocks in first, you'll never get them in at all."

So what are the big rocks? Of all the things that clamor for our time, energy, and attention—what matters most? Someone once asked Jesus that question. In Mark 12 a religious leader asked Jesus, "What is the greatest commandment?" In short, this religious leader was asking Jesus, "What are the big rocks? What matters most?"

Week 3: Jesus' Grace: Am I Accepted?

Matthew 9:10–13; John 8:1–11

As noted earlier, don't be afraid to use content from this chapter for your sermon. For example, I highly recommend that you tell Tony Campolo's story about Agnes. I've heard and told this story many times, and it still deeply moves me. Remember, repetition is a good thing!

The text for week 3 is John 8:1–11. Most scholars doubt that this story was in the earliest manuscripts of the Gospel of John. However, since this story is burned into the "canon" of most people and since it's so much like Jesus, I don't worry about that. However, if you don't want to use this text, many others illustrate Jesus' grace, including Matthew 9:10–13.

When I preached this sermon at my church, we showed a video clip depicting the story of the woman caught in adultery from the old movie *Jesus of Nazareth*. You can get that clip at www.wingclips.com. Look under the topic "judging," and then find *Jesus of Nazareth*. The clip is called "First Stone." It lasts just under three minutes.

Consider building your sermon in the following way. Begin with the C. S. Lewis, Anne Lamott, and/or Will Campbell story from the first few pages of chapter 13. Then move to the text. Add your own thoughts and experiences of grace. Then conclude with the Campolo story.

Week 4: Jesus' Work: Where Is God?

John 1:1–5, 14

This week you and your congregation will grapple with the question Where is God? Another way of asking the question is, "How does God work in the world?" The answer is that God works through people, as we clearly see in the incarnation of Christ.

Once again, don't be hesitant to use materials from chapter 14 of the book. For example, the chapter lists numerous biblical examples of God's using people to do God's work in the world. And the humorous closing story about God sending a "professional" can be used effectively as either the introduction or conclusion of the sermon.

The most important part of week 4's sermon is *your own local experience of God at work*. You need to share where you see God at work in the world, especially in the life of your congregation and community. You don't need dramatic stories. You just need to share examples of God's working through the people in your congregation. For example, if I were preaching this sermon at my church this Sunday, I'd tell about last week's barbecue event at my church. One of our young adult Sunday school classes cooked a huge amount of BBQ, sold it to members of the church and the community, and used the proceeds to support inner-city ministry with children. The week before, another Sunday school class rallied around a member going through chemotherapy. They sent her notes, brought her food, cleaned her house, and mowed her yard. These events were simple yet powerful examples of God's working through human instruments in our local church and community. These kinds of local examples of God at work in your community will mean far more to your folks than stories from my book or any-place else.

That being the case, I can't offer many more preaching helps for this Sunday. However, the following story, while silly, might serve as a good introduction to your sermon:

Where Is God?

A young mother was at wit's end with her two boys, ages eight and ten. The boys constantly engaged in mischief. Through the grapevine this mother heard that the local Catholic priest had great success in disciplining children. So she asked him if he would speak with her boys. The priest agreed but asked to see them individually. The next morning the mother sent her eight-year-old to see the priest, with the older boy scheduled to see him that afternoon.

The priest, a huge man with a booming voice, sat the younger boy down in the sanctuary, then asked him sternly, "Where is God?"

The boy's mouth dropped open, but he made no response. He just stared at the priest, wide-eyed, with his mouth hanging open.

So the priest repeated the question in even a sterner tone: "Where is God?"

Again the boy made no attempt to answer.

So the priest raised his voice even more, shook his finger in the boy's face, and shouted, "WHERE IS GOD?"

The boy screamed at the top of his lungs, bolted from the church, ran home, and dove into his bedroom closet, slamming the door behind him.

His older brother rushed to the bedroom and said, "What happened?"

The younger brother, gasping for breath, replied, "We're in *big* trouble this time. God is missing, and they think *we* did it!"

It's a silly story but an important question. Where is God? Where is God at work in the world? *Is* God at work in the world? The answer surely is yes. God is at work all over the world, primarily through human instruments.

Week 5: Jesus' Example: What Brings Fulfillment?

John 13:1–5, 13–17

Week 5 reminds people that true meaning and fulfillment in life come from serving others. The text, from John 13, tells the story of Jesus' washing the disciples' feet. As Jesus said in this text, when we follow his example and serve other people, we "will be blessed" (v. 17 NIV).

There are several stories in chapter 15 that you can use in your sermon. Almost everyone is familiar with Habitat for Humanity, so the Millard Fuller story is a good one to tell. The closing story about Gus is powerful, so you should give serious consideration to using it. You might also want to use the Mark Green story from *ER*, "Dr. Green's Final Prescription." If you have projection capability, you can find the clip on Season 8 of *ER*, "On the Beach" (November 13, 2008).

A good flow for the sermon would be to begin with the Millard Fuller story, then move to the text, and close with the Gus story. Of course, you can add your own experiences and stories as well. In case you need it, an additional extended story on the theme of service follows:

Christmas at First Church

Several years ago, a United Methodist Church in North Carolina learned about the joy of service, both individually and as a congregation. This church, concerned about homeless people in their town, especially during the winter months, spearheaded a program to help. They, along with fourteen other churches in their city, committed to care for homeless people for one week each winter. Each church opened up its facilities, usually the fellowship hall, to care for about eighteen to twenty homeless guests. Their job was to provide them with a warm and safe place to sleep, meals, and other needs for the entire week.

In early November the cooperating churches had their final organizational meeting. The purpose of the meeting was to schedule a specific week for each church for the winter months. The United Methodist pastor planned to go to the meeting, but she was busy, so she asked a woman from her church to go in her place. This woman, a new Christian and new church member, was an enthusiastic and devoted layperson. The pastor gave her a list of convenient weeks in January and February for their congregation to care for the homeless group. The pastor told her, "Make sure to schedule us for one of these weeks."

The woman went to the meeting. But not long into the meeting, they reached an impasse. Not one of the fifteen cooperating churches was willing to take Christmas week. First, it interfered with all their Christmas activities, including Christmas Eve services. Second, everybody knew that their members would not want to cook meals and provide other services for homeless folks during the Christmas holidays. This woman, an enthusiastic new Christian believer, was dumbfounded. She could not believe that none of the churches would take Christmas week. The more they argued about who was going to have to take Christmas, the madder this woman got.

Before she knew it, she smashed her hand down on the table, stood up, and gave a speech. "I can't believe this," she exclaimed. "Jesus and his family were homeless in Bethlehem on the very first Christmas, and yet not one church in this community is willing to care for homeless people during the week of Christmas. Shame on you!"

The pastors all felt ashamed but not ashamed enough to volunteer for the week of Christmas! When nobody volunteered, this laywoman boldly proclaimed, "My church, the First United Methodist Church, will take Christmas week, not only this year but every year."

One of the pastors said, "So moved."

Another said, "I'll second that." After a quick vote, the meeting adjourned.

After the meeting was over, this woman went to see her pastor. She was excited. She said, "I have great news! Our church gets to care for homeless people during the week of Christmas, not only this year but every year! Isn't that great?"

Well, that wasn't exactly great news to the pastor. What about their Christmas Eve services? How would they find volunteers to cook and care for homeless people during the holidays? No, this was not good news at all to the pastor. In fact, she was sorry she had not gone to the meeting herself. But what could she do? It was a done deal.

The next Sunday the pastor gave the news to her congregation. She said, "We are going to host homeless people during the week of Christmas, and we need a bunch of volunteers to help."

She didn't think she would get any response, but she was wrong. People came out of the woodwork to volunteer. Families with young children volunteered, saying to the pastor, "We want our kids to know there is more to

Christmas than getting presents." Families who had lost loved ones during the year volunteered, hoping to fill the void of the Christmas season. In fact, the pastor got more volunteers than she could use. Christmas week finally arrived. Eighteen homeless people came to the Methodist church to spend the week. And much to this pastor's surprise, it ended up being the highlight of the year for the church.

People brought in tons of food all week long. The homeless guests ate like kings all week. Church members also brought nice clothes and coats for them to wear. They brought gifts for everyone, especially the children. And they didn't just give food and clothes and gifts; they gave of themselves as well. People stayed for hours to visit with the group. They ate meals with them and played games with them. They even had a marathon, three-day-long Monopoly tournament! Many members spent one or more nights during the week. The church members got to know these people as *real* people.

Although they were not required to go, all eighteen of the homeless guests went to the Christmas Eve Candlelight Communion service. They were warmly welcomed by the entire congregation, and everyone in attendance had a holy moment. In fact, the whole week turned out to be a glorious experience for the church, and it continued to be that way for the next five years.

This story has an unusual ending. After six years of hosting homeless folks during the week of Christmas, the Methodist pastor got a phone call from the Baptist pastor. He said, "You know, everyone in this town has heard about how much fun your church has hosting the homeless group at Christmas. So we were wondering, would you be willing to share that week with some of the other churches? We were hoping we could do Christmas week this year."

This United Methodist Church in North Carolina learned something profound through this experience. They learned that true fulfillment comes not by taking care of our own needs but by taking care of others' needs. May that be true in your life and in mine.

Week 6: Jesus' Death: What about Suffering?

Matthew 27:27–31

This week your congregation will grapple with the problem of suffering. Three preaching options follow:

1. Stick closely to the book. Chapter 16 provides more than ample preaching material. Pick a few sections of the chapter to use, add an experience from your own life about finding God in suffering, and conclude with the final story about David and the crucifix. This will work well.

2. Forgo a regular sermon. Instead, do a combination of Scripture readings and a solo. This will work best if your seven-week series occurs during the season of Lent. If so, week 6 will fall on Palm/Passion Sunday. (Another option is to do this Scripture/song approach on Good Friday.) After introducing the theme of suffering, you will read selected Scriptures from the passion of Jesus. Between segments of the readings, a soloist will sing three verses (a cappella) of "Were You There?" Here's the way it would look:

Introduction

Many of you have heard of Elie Wiesel. Wiesel, a Jew, is a survivor of the holocaust. During his teenage years he and his family were imprisoned at Auschwitz, the infamous Nazi concentration camp. Other than himself, everyone in Elie Wiesel's family perished in that horrible camp. In one of his books, Wiesel tells a powerful story from his experience at Auschwitz. The story involves a hanging that he and all the prisoners were forced to witness. Three men were hung by the Nazis, one of them just a teenage boy. They had been accused of blowing up a power station.

To warn the other inmates of the high cost of resistance, all the inmates were forced to walk by and see the execution at close range. It was a grisly scene—a scene of death, evil, and suffering. By the time Wiesel marched by, the two adults were dead. But the youth was still alive, hanging on the gallows, struggling between life and death. Behind him Wiesel heard a man ask: "Where is God now? Where is he?"

That's the question, isn't it? Where is God? Where is God in my illness? Where is God as I face the reality of death? Where is God as I face a deteriorating marriage, financial problems, doubt, and depression? Where is God in the midst of war, terrorism, earthquakes, fear, and hatred?

The execution continued. The lad lingered on. Once again Elie heard the man ask, "Where is God?"

Elie Wiesel said, "I heard a voice within me answer him: *Where is God? He is there, hanging on the gallows.*"

The cross of Jesus tells us that God is a God of the gallows, a crucified God. Although God does not take away our suffering, God enters into our pain and shares it with us. The Bible foretells that Jesus is "a man of sorrows, acquainted with grief." The cross tells us that when we suffer, God suffers with us. So on this Passion Sunday [or Good Friday], let us remember that our God is a crucified God.

Scripture Readings/Solo

Read Mark 14:22–24, 26–27, 29–37, 41–43, 45–46, 50.
Soloist sings first stanza: "Were you there when they crucified my Lord?"

Read Mark 14:53, 55, 60–65; 15:1, 12–20.
Soloist sings second stanza: "Were you there when they nailed him to the tree?"

Read Mark 15:25–32; Luke 23:34; Mark 15:33–34; Luke 23:46.
Soloist sings third stanza: "Were you there when they laid him in the tomb?"

3. A third preaching option is to use the above Elie Wiesel story as a brief devotional, drop the Scripture/song combination, and observe Holy Communion.

Week 7: Jesus' Resurrection: Is There Hope?

Matthew 28:1–7

The theme for week 7, based on chapter 17, is hope. If you do this series during Lent, week 7 will fall on Easter

Sunday. However, any Sunday of the year is a good day to celebrate the great hope of Christ's resurrection.

Like weeks 1–6, you can find plenty of preaching material for week 7 in the book. For example, you might want to tell "The Last Word Is Hope" story from the movie *The Shawshank Redemption*. If you have projection capability, consider showing the following two clips: (1) 71:27–72:56 and (2) 134:30–136:15, immediately followed by 136:56–138:13.

The following story of resurrection hope would also work well:

Are We Having Easter This Year?

Back in March 1994, a young woman named Kelly Clem was serving as the pastor of Goshen United Methodist Church in Piedmont, Alabama. The Sunday before Easter, Palm Sunday, the church was packed. Kelly's two-year-old daughter, Sarah, was in the church nursery. Kelly's four-year-old daughter, Hannah, was dressed in a little blue-and-white choir robe, sitting on the front row with the children's choir.

As the service got under way, the congregation heard wind blowing outside. The sky turned black. Then the lightning began, followed by hail. Suddenly there was a burst of wind. The stained-glass window shattered, and shards of glass shot across the sanctuary. Somebody shouted, "Tornado!" Pieces of ceiling started to fall. There was a horrible sound as the roof of the church was ripped off, and the building crashed around them.

Reverend Kelly ran to check on her children. But a brick hit her on the head, and she fell hard on her shoulder. When she finally got up, she looked around at the devastation. Someone told her that her two-year-old daughter, Sarah, was OK—that the nursery was still intact.

Then Kelly looked down to where her four-year-old daughter, Hannah, had been sitting. There was nothing there but a pile of bricks. Under that pile of bricks, she could see little blue-and-white choir robes. Members of the church pulled Hannah and the other children out of the bricks, but Hannah did not make it. Nineteen people in the church died, and eighty-six others were injured.

Over the next few days, Kelly performed one funeral after another, including one for her daughter. Toward the end of that awful week, Kelly began receiving phone calls from members of the congregation. Given the death of the pastor's daughter and the destruction of their sanctuary, they asked, "Reverend Clem, are we having Easter this year?"

But Kelly knew they weren't just asking about Sunday's services. She knew they were saying, "Reverend Clem, we desperately *need* Easter." And after leading nineteen funerals, including the funeral of her four-year-old daughter, Kelly Clem knew that *she* needed Easter also. So Kelly and her congregation planned an Easter sunrise service.

A few days after the tornado, a reporter asked Reverend Clem if the disaster had shattered her faith. She replied: "It has not shattered my faith. I'm holding on to my faith. It's holding me. All of the people of Goshen are holding on to one another, along with the hope that they will be able to rebuild." Then Kelly said to the reporter, "Easter is coming."

That Sunday morning at the Easter sunrise service, two hundred people gathered in the front yard of the destroyed facilities at Goshen UMC. With a bandage on her head, her shoulder in a brace, and her heart breaking

with grief, Reverend Kelly made her way to the make-
shift pulpit. She opened her Bible, looked into the faces
of her traumatized congregation, and then read these
words from Romans 8: "Nothing in all creation can sep-
arate us from the love of God in Christ Jesus our Lord."

A MESSAGE TO PASTORS

If you enjoyed the content and storytelling style of this book and Study Guide, you will want to visit the author's preaching and worship Web site at www .GettingReadyForSunday.com. The site includes preaching, worship, and pastoral leadership articles, sermons and sermon series, Martin's columns in *Net Results* magazine and MinistryMatters.com, and other helpful information for clergy.

Other Books by Martin Thielen

Getting Ready for Sunday: A Practical Guide
for Worship Planning

Getting Ready for Sunday's Sermon:
A Practical Guide for Sermon Preparation

Getting Ready for Special Sundays:
A Practical Guide for Worship
and Preaching Preparation

Ancient-Modern Worship:
A Practical Guide to Blending Worship Styles

CPSIA information can be obtained
at www.ICGtesting.com
Printed in the USA
BVHW070359230321
603013BV00014B/105

9 780664 239381